BOOKS BY KENNETH S. DAVIS

NONFICTION

Invincible Summer: An Intimate Portrait of the Roosevelts (1974)

FDR: The Beckoning of Destiny, 1882–1928, A History (1972)

The Politics of Honor, a biography of Adlai E. Stevenson (1967)

The Cautionary Scientists:
Priestley, Lavoisier, and the Founding of Modern Chemistry (1966)

Experience of War: The U.S. in World War II (1965)

Water: The Mirror of Science WITH JOHN A. DAY (1961)

The Hero: Charles A. Lindbergh and the American Dream (1959)

A Prophet in His Own Country:
The Triumphs and Defeats of Adlai E. Stevenson (1957)

River on the Rampage (1953)

Soldier of Democracy, a biography of Dwight D. Eisenhower (1945)

NOVELS

Morning in Kansas (1952)

The Years of the Pilgrimage (1948)

In the Forests of the Night (1942)

INVINCIBLE SUMMER

INVINCIBLE SUMMER

An Intimate Portrait of

THE ROOSEVELTS

based on the recollections of

MARION DICKERMAN

BY KENNETH S. DAVIS

This book was prepared and developed with the assistance of Mary Belle Starr

ATHENEUM

NEW YORK

1974

All photographs and illustrative material in this book,
unless credited otherwise,
are from the private collection of Marion Dickerman.

In memory of
NANCY COOK

"In the depths of winter,
I finally learned that within
me there lay an invincible summer."

Albert Camus

AUTHOR'S NOTE

M ANY IMPORTANT biographies and histories of recent years derived much of their subject matter from the rich resources of Columbia University's Oral History Research Office, but the present work is perhaps unique in that its very genesis was in that office. It is also unusual in that, like a play or motion picture, it may be said to have a producer as well as an author and publisher.

A few years ago, Mary Belle Starr, wife of the director of the Research Office, made the acquaintance of Miss Marion Dickerman. Out of this acquaintanceship grew tape-recorded interviews of Miss Dickerman by Mrs. Starr for Oral History, in the course of which the two became close friends. When Mrs. Starr learned that her interview subject possessed many hours of motion pictures of the family life of the Franklin Roosevelts—candid home movies never seen by the public, taken by Miss Dickerman's friend Nancy Cook—she persuaded the National Broadcasting Company to put together from them a TV Chronolog production, which was nationally broadcast in 1972.

Out of this project grew in Mrs. Starr's mind the idea that an interesting and historically valuable book might be made of frames from the motion pictures as well as of some of the hundreds of unpublished still photographs in Miss Dickerman's possession. She persuaded Miss Dickerman that this was so. She interested Alfred Knopf, Jr., of Atheneum in her idea. She and Mr. Knopf asked me to write the accompanying text. And she subsequently helped to select the pictures used and to write the captions and prepare the index.

The book we now present differs considerably from the initial idea for it. As I studied the transcripts of Miss Dickerman's Oral History interviews, had repeated lengthy interviews with her myself, and reviewed the intimate correspondence between her and Nancy Cook with both FDR and Eleanor Roosevelt, I realized that something more substantial than a mere "accompanying" text was called for—and with this conclusion Miss Dickerman and Mrs. Starr quickly agreed. Hence writing the book has not been the easy task I envisaged at the outset. It has been an enriching experience for me, however—and in no small part because of the personal friendship it has enabled me to form with two remarkable women.

KENNETH S. DAVIS, *Princeton, Massachusetts*

CONTENTS

A NOTE ON THE PICTURES

The forty pages of photographs and memorabilia selected for the album appearing in this book (following page 65) were drawn exclusively from the private collection of Marion Dickerman. With a few exceptions, the photographs presented here were taken by Miss Dickerman's close friend and associate, Nancy Cook. Since Miss Cook also recorded many memorable occasions with a movie camera, some of the album's pictures are still frames taken from 16-millimeter motion-picture film. Most of this material has never been published before.

PRELUDE

ON
SUNSET
HILL

T H E   P A S T as memory fills up vacant spaces in the present. It becomes more vivid as the present becomes more dully monotonous, repetitious, empty of novel experience; it grows more insistent in its claims upon conscious attention as its bulk increases and the amount of individual future shrinks inexorably toward zero. As we grow older, therefore, we find ourselves living more and more in the past; and few would deny that pathos invests this substitution of a remembered for an actual life. To the young it seems wholly sad.

Nevertheless, the transaction is by no means a dead loss.

The reduction in vital excitements is offset by a gain in knowledge and wisdom. Reliving the past we come to know it as we never did and never could have done when the past was a present experience. We come to a better understanding of its events, the people in it, and our own potential (now actual) selves. Nor is this understanding limited to the past as a completed business. Of its very essence is the perception of an underlying pattern that extends through all the time between then and now, and of which the present moment, as it ceaselessly works into the future, seems in some sense to be a "working out." This pattern is historically useful. It provides standards for the assessment of values, for the measurement of relative importance, not just among the events and people of the past but among those of the present day, and by implication, the days yet to come.

Marion Dickerman is a tall gray-haired woman, slender, slightly stooped, but in a way that seems less indicative of physical infirmity than of a courteous deference to those shorter than she; indeed, she retains, to a surprising degree, the bodily vigor along with the emotional and intellectual resiliency of youth. Her face, like the rest of her physical self, is long and narrow. Its lines are quite severely vertical, so that, insofar as the horizontal is expressive of jollity while the vertical is expressive of sadness, she has in repose a somewhat sorrowful countenance. Her eyes, however, are nearly always bright: on occasion they light her face into a smile that is beautiful to see; and in general she maintains, seemingly undiminished, the essentially optimistic idealism of that Progressive Era in which she grew up. She does not do so out of ignorance of what is now going on. She is keenly aware of current social, cultural, and—above all—political affairs, and reacts to their salient features with a range and intensity of feeling as great as a young person's, though tempered in her case by a sense of recurrent pattern, an awareness of resonance.

But the fact remains: she is not young, nor does she ever claim that her years are any fewer than they actually are. This particular vanity would be denied her in any case by the fact that, for forty years and more, *Who's Who in America* has told all who cared to know that Marion Dickerman was born in Westfield, New York, on April 11, 1890, attended Wellesley in 1907–1909, and received her A.B. from Syracuse in 1911, with advanced degrees in education from that same university a year later. In following years and decades she became nationally known as an educator, a leader of women's activities in the Democratic party, and a specialist in labor relations. For seventeen years (1945–1962) she was educational director of the famous Marine Museum of Mystic, Connecticut.

Since 1947 her home has been a charming and quite commodious French-style country house at 33 Sunset Hill Road in New Canaan—an address that strikes her calm sense of temporal realities as peculiarly apt. From this house, through the living room's picture window, by which she breakfasts and lunches every day, she looks out upon a formal garden, classically austere in the French style. On one side it is bounded by the wings of the house (flaming fire thorn warms the wall

4

when winter snows bury the garden) and on the other three by a box hedge, neatly trimmed, against which, at the garden's bottom, stands a three-foot-high bronze figure of an infant holding a turtle in either hand. The garden, for Marion, is one of memories. It was made by her lifelong friend and companion, Nancy Cook.

Marion first met Nancy in a student boarding house where they both lived in Syracuse, in the fall of 1909. Nancy was some seven years older than Marion and several inches shorter—an intense, vivid, crisp-mannered girl with bright curly hair and brown eyes that were always sharply outward-looking and seemed sometimes literally to crackle and blaze with electric energy. Considerably less "intellectual" than Marion, she displayed a no more than average talent for symbolic manipulations, whether of language or mathematics, and had slight interest in the abstract or theoretical. Her intelligence was creatively practical: it flowed out through remarkably sensitive, beautifully controlled fingers. She could "do almost anything with her hands," Eleanor Roosevelt once wrote of her.

In general, she lived at a faster pace, under greater pressure, than Marion. A high nervous tension (it shows in her photographed face, which is always tense and often frowningly so) caused her to vibrate at high frequency. And this was stimulating to Marion; it heightened her awareness, and quickened a vital tempo that was slow, or sometimes seemed so, compared to Nancy's. Nancy, in her turn, could lean and draw upon Marion's reserves and healthfully moderate an often excessive quickness and impatience in terms of Marion's greater steadiness, rhythmic regularity, and steadfastness of purpose. Thus the two complemented one another; they sensed this almost at once. Soon they had become the fastest of friends, bound together forever by ties of mutual inward need.

While at Syracuse the two became ardent suffragettes, determined not only to win the vote for women but to participate actively themselves in politics, battling for clean government, world peace (they were pacifists as a matter of course), the abolition of child labor, the protection of women against industrial exploitation. And they carried

5

this idealism into their teaching in the school system of Fulton, New York, when they went there together in 1913—Marion to teach American history and social studies in the high school, Nancy to teach art and handicrafts. By then they were both dedicated followers of Woodrow Wilson. When the United States entered the First World War, the two girls plunged into local war-related organizational work—the Red Cross, the Liberty Loan drives—despite their pacifism. Or perhaps in part because of it. For "we really believed this was a war to end wars and make the world safe for democracy," as Marion recalls.

Meanwhile they pulled strings to be accepted as staff members of the Endell Street Hospital in London, which, with two exceptions, was staffed entirely by women. They went abroad in the spring of 1918 "with the distinct understanding that we were not nurses and would have nothing to do with the care of wounded men but would scrub floors or perform whatever other chores were required." They arrived in Endell Street, however, simultaneously with scores of gravely wounded men, far more than the hospital was staffed to handle, and perforce accepted assignment as nursing orderlies in two of the most critical wards in the hospital.

Marion managed to harden herself sufficiently to endure the sights and sounds of extreme human agony and to work among them effectively. But Nancy simply could not do so. Her phenomenal skill with her hands was frustrated by an excessive empathy: her physical recoil from a suffering she felt all too acutely was uncontrollable, so that she, normally so precise and delicate in her manual operations, became almost clumsy in situations where delicate precision was urgently necessary. She begged for another assignment. So when the order went out that no man who had lost a leg was to be discharged from the hospital until he had been fitted with his first artificial one, she was sent to learn how to make artificial legs. She became an expert in a mere twelve lessons. Thereafter, for as long as she and Marion remained in Endell Street, she made every artificial leg that was fitted to a discharged patient.

Not until August 1919 did the two return to America.

6

By then women had won the right to vote in New York. A Joint Legislative Conference had been organized "by a group of outstanding women and a few men" in the state for purposes of governmental reform and the promotion of liberal welfare legislation. Chief obstacle to the passage of such legislation was the extremely reactionary Republican assemblyman from Oswego County (in which Fulton is located) who, as Assembly Speaker, was ex officio head of the Republican caucus. And Marion discovered to her utter astonishment, upon landing in New York City, that she had been slated by the conference to run as Democratic candidate in the 1919 election against this powerful opponent. The odds against her winning such a race were overwhelming. Nevertheless, after some soul-searching, she submitted to what was in effect a draft, becoming the first woman ever to run for the New York legislature. She lost, of course. But with Nancy as her campaign manager she ran much stronger than she had been expected to do and thereby denied her opponent the Republican gubernatorial nomination to which he had aspired.

For Nancy Cook's subsequent career this campaign was decisive. Political activity was filled with tingling combative excitement that made teaching seem to her comparatively dull and tame. She therefore gave up teaching without a qualm—she had no school contract for that year anyway—when Harriet May Mills, whom she had met in Syracuse, and whom she and Marion liked and admired, asked her in early 1920 to help organize the new Women's Division of the New York Democratic party. Democratic politics was to be her major professional activity ever after.

Marion remained in education. She served a restive year as dean at the New Jersey State Normal School in Trenton in 1920–1921, then taught in Bryn Mawr's summer school in 1922 before entering upon what was to be the major phase of her professional career. But of her life also the campaign in 1919 was in many ways decisive, for it soon led her and Nancy, through Nancy's work, into a friendship with Eleanor Roosevelt that was of immense importance to all three of them personally and of some importance, too, in American history.

The house on Sunset Hill Road is richly furnished with memories of this friendship. Tangible memories. The table at which Marion sits for lunch before the picture window is a handcrafted piece of early American design so beautifully finished that the wood glows softly in one's sight and is as velvet to one's touch. It was made in the once-famous Val-Kill Industries shop, which Marion, Nancy, and Eleanor owned together. So was most of the other furniture in the house. All the walls are hung with memorabilia of the Roosevelt years—inscribed photographs, watercolors, oil paintings, framed letters. Everywhere that Marion looks in her home she sees the past. And sometimes, looking out her picture window into the garden in the spring and summer, she sees the past there, too, so vivid that it blots out the present. She sees Nancy moving there with rake or trowel in hand, leaning over the flower beds—though Nancy has been dead, now, for a dozen years. Seeing Nancy she also sees young junipers aspiring above the bottom hedge, though they are no longer actually there, having been cut down years ago because they had grown so tall they shaded the garden and blocked the view beyond. The view is open now. A wide sky spreads its moods above a wide acre of meadow with a stand of hardwood at its far end, across which flows for Marion a various wind of memory, sometimes harsh and bitter cold but more often warm, gentle, and sweetly, sadly scented by a mingling of the nostalgic with green-growing things.

PART ONE

VAL KILL COTTAGE

O N E

IN EARLY summer of 1922, Marion Dickerman and Nancy Cook started out on a vacation automobile tour of their native up-state New York, during which they would stop for visits with scattered friends and relatives. On the way northward they paused, on a Friday afternoon, at Mrs. Gordon Norrie's home, a large and beautiful estate, in the Hudson River town of Staatsburg. Mrs. Norrie was a wealthy woman, fervent in her commitment to idealistic causes, who had contributed handsomely in money and also in time and energy to Marion's 1919 election campaign. She had at that time become a warm friend of Marion's and Nancy's. She was also a close friend of Eleanor and Franklin Roosevelt of Hyde Park, which was the next town south of Staatsburg; and on this Friday afternoon she spoke casually of the pleasure she took in the fact that Marion and Nancy were spending that weekend with the Roosevelts.

"What makes you think that?" asked Nancy, in astonishment.

"Why, Eleanor told me you were, just this morning. I saw her in the market."

"But we haven't been asked," Nancy said.

Whereupon Mrs. Norrie phoned Eleanor, who, it turned out, had mailed a letter of invitation that had not been received and who now, when the phone was turned over to Nancy, begged the two vacationers to accept.

And so, within a couple of hours thereafter, having driven southward on the Albany Post Road through Hyde Park village, Marion made for the first time in her life a turn she and Nancy were later to make thousands of times—a turn between two brownstone gateposts and down a long, tree-lined drive at whose end, where the level land broke into a long, wooded slope to the river, a handsome Georgian mansion stood. Out onto the steps of its semicircular porch, as the car approached, came a tall slender woman whose countenance in repose had a blunt, almost an aggressive plainness—an effect due, perhaps, to protuberant front teeth, which made her chin seem to recede. She appeared at first glance somewhat older than her actual thirty-eight years. But then the car came to a halt; she came down the steps with welcoming hand outstretched, her face lighted by a smile that radiated from large, lovely eyes and drew her wide lips apart, so that her large, white, even teeth flashed quite handsomely in the late afternoon sunlight, and all at once she seemed attractively young, and eager. She was, in fact, glowing.

"Nancy!" she cried, in a rather high-pitched but not unmusical voice. "How good to see you again!"

And then Nancy introduced Marion to Eleanor Roosevelt.

The first meeting between Nancy and Eleanor had taken place several months before.

At that time, in the spring of 1922, Nancy as executive secretary of the Women's Division of the Democratic State Committee had been arranging a huge fund-raising luncheon and was in quest of a potent

12

crowd-attracting "name" to preside over the affair, to be held in a midtown hotel. At that same time, Eleanor was in the midst of a slow process of emergence from a prolonged and severely testing crisis in her life. She was reaching out for new activities that would serve her husband's interests, helping both in his spiritual and political recovery from the disastrous effects of his polio attack of the previous summer; and that also would encourage in her the healthy growth of a strong independent self out of a self that had been too much dependent on others and, by these others, had been gravely injured. Nancy's immediate quest and Eleanor's long-term need met in happy fusion: when the executive secretary, having thought of Mrs. Franklin D. Roosevelt as the perfect "name" for the luncheon chairmanship, telephoned the Roosevelt home at 49 East Sixty-fifth Street, Eleanor quickly agreed to do what Nancy wanted. She did so despite the fact she "had never done anything for a political organization before" nor "ever made a speech to any sizable gathering" and had not "the faintest idea of what I was going to say or what the organization was really doing," as she later wrote.

Not until the day of the luncheon did she and Nancy meet face to face. By then, however, a remarkable rapport seems to have been already established between them, through their telephone conversations.

Eleanor arrived at the hotel carrying a bunch of violets. "Where is Miss Cook?" she asked, as almost her first words. And when Nancy was presented to her, she presented the violets to Nancy—a gesture of poignant sweetness for the younger woman, and for Marion, too, when Marion learned of it. As for the luncheon, it was a great success. Eleanor did far better than she had thought she could do, and was heartened thereby to continue with her new departure. From that day forward to the last of her days she would be always deeply and actively involved in Democratic political organization.

Soon afterward she invited Nancy to spend a weekend at Hyde Park—a weekend Nancy had since described to Marion in glowing detail.

13

So Marion was somewhat prepared psychologically, on this sunny afternoon, for her sudden, unexpected immersion in the Roosevelt family life. Nevertheless, the experience astonished and delighted her, and it yet remains vivid in her living memory as the first unit of a new kind of time, a time of stronger rhythms, greater thickness, and a more richly various texture than any she had known before.

There was such a surging abundance of life at Hyde Park!

Only half the Roosevelt family were there that weekend. The head of the family was not; the three older children were not. Even so, Marion's first impression was a confused blur, a welter of moving colors and sounds. But very soon the blurred confusion yielded up a pattern whose foci were distinctively individual people, for though the Roosevelts were all alike in their possession of, or being possessed by, a restless overflow of energy, each of them, save the chief one who was absent that day, had a sharp clear outline, and all of them, including this absent one, had a defining effect upon the people with whom they came in contact. Thus Marion soon clearly identified the two handsome children—six-year-old John and eight-year-old Franklin, Jr.—as they contributed hugely to the bustling confusion by dashing in and out of the house and across the wide lawns in pursuit of active pleasures.

She identified at once and unmistakably a large, regal, elderly lady (she was sixty-eight) whom the children called Granny and whom Eleanor called Granny, too, though she was introduced as Mrs. James (Sara Delano) Roosevelt. Eleanor's mother-in-law was clearly the matriarch here—a gracious lady but also a formidable one whose manner, if always flawlessly courteous, was not always designed to put others at ease. Many found her intimidating. Her broad, firm-chinned countenance was pleasant enough, even charming when she smiled, but the habit of command sat upon it, and to most eyes it retained few traces of the softly feminine and slenderly sculptured beauty that had once been hers. Marion, however, found her attractive and liked her from the first. She appealed strongly to the traditional, the conservative in Marion's character. "She came out of a different world, was an almost perfect example of upper-class Victorian woman and had most

14

of the Victorian attitudes and prejudices," Marion admits, "and since she was certainly strong-willed she could be difficult. But I never found her so. I found her always a warm and kind friend. I think she suffered much from being misunderstood, though she was too much of an aristocrat ever to show it."

But Marion sensed that the central focus of all the whirl of activity at Hyde Park, even on that weekend of his physical absence, was neither Granny nor Eleanor but Granny's son, Eleanor's husband. Certainly it was around him that virtually all of Granny's conversation revolved, and to him Eleanor's again and again reverted.

Inevitably much of the talk was political. Franklin Roosevelt was beginning to make political news again after the long silence imposed on him by his polio attack. He had issued an open letter to Al Smith, begging that worthy to accept the Democratic nomination for Governor of New York. Running for reelection, Smith as governor had been defeated by Nathan Miller in 1920, but by a margin so narrow as to amount to a personal triumph, measured against the tremendous proportions of that year's Republican landslide. Clearly, Smith had an excellent chance for victory in 1922—and he had just replied in an open letter to "Dear Frank" that he would indeed run. Eleanor and her husband, with the unenthusiastic acquiescence of Granny, were planning to hold a big reception for him here in Hyde Park in early September.

Roosevelt himself, though he was said to be steadily "improving," was in no shape to campaign actively that fall, but Nancy and Eleanor would be deeply involved, as would Marion be, to the degree permitted by a teaching commitment she had just made. And all of them knew this that weekend, for the two principal managers of Smith's electioneering, Joseph M. Proskauer and Mrs. Belle Moskowitz, had already indicated their intention to make extensive use, for the first time in any campaign, of the Democratic party's new Women's Division.

Eleanor, moreover—with whom, it seemed now certain, Marion and Nancy were thenceforth to be intimate friends—was being pushed ever more deeply into political work by her husband's (and her own) great friend, Louis Howe, who was also her husband's closest working associate.

By the time she and Nancy drove away, up the long, maple-lined driveway to the Albany Post Road, late Sunday afternoon, Marion had a clear sense that a new and immensely expanded life, full of the greatest excitement, was opening out before her, and that Hyde Park was to be a major center, perhaps *the* center, of her future.

When next they came to Hyde Park, as they did very soon, they found all the Roosevelt children there. To the boisterous activity of John and Franklin, Jr., was added that of fourteen-year-old James and twelve-year-old Elliott, each with a friend or two in tow and accompanied by frequently yelping dogs. More sedate, as befitted a practically full-grown young lady, was sixteen-year-old Anna, the eldest child, the only daughter. Yet she, too, was intensely, energetically alive, animated of voice and vividly expressive of face—a remarkably pretty face—as she tossed her shining, shoulder-length blond hair this way and that in gestures often as communicative as her words.

And Franklin Delano Roosevelt was there.

Later, as she sorted out her first impressions of him, Marion was shocked by the recognition that he was totally crippled. The general impression conveyed by the press had been that he was only mildly handicapped, able to get about, if limpingly, and would walk again soon without any limp whatever. Nor was this impression contradicted by Marion's initial experience of him. He simply remained seated. Only afterward was it borne in upon her that he couldn't walk at all! His legs, which Marion would later often see as he sat in a swimsuit at a pool's edge, were withered from the hips downward. Only with the help of others could he swing himself from bed to wheelchair, from wheelchair to sofa or armchair; only with steel braces strapped to his sticklike limbs and crutches under his arms could he come anywhere near even a semblance of walking, and doing so required in that summer an enormous, sweating effort that Marion was not permitted to see. Otherwise he had to push himself in a wheelchair, or be pushed,

16

to get from one place to another, and if there were steps he had to be lifted and carried by brawny men.

Yet he did not *seem* a cripple, even after one recognized that he was. The shock of such recognition was acute because it was so discordant with one's general sense of him, and it wore off quickly. Within a few minutes one had forgotten about Roosevelt's legs, had lost all awareness of his physical disability. He had not yet fully developed, in that summer, the thick neck, the huge, iron-hard shoulders, the tremendous breadth of chest, the heavily muscled torso that were later his; but he bulked large in his wheelchair and was obviously, from the waist up, a physically powerful man. He had a large head and a handsome, finely chiseled face, broad of cheek and jut-jawed, and when he smiled broadly (his smile was frequent and radiant) he showed teeth that, though uneven, were strong and white. He had absolutely none of the sick man's psychology—not a trace of self-pity or of the petulance, the overt and covert demands upon the sympathies of others, that so often characterize the handicapped. Indeed, the overall impression he gave was of robust good health, of glowing energy, of immense *joie de vivre.* Waves of vital force, of magnetic force, radiated from him and drew others strongly toward him. He seemed to make things happen around him, effortlessly, by means of sheer immobile presence.

Never in her life before had Marion met so utterly charming a man. It at once seemed to her perfectly right and natural that people should devote themselves heart and soul to him and his career.

Among those doing so, whom Marion then met for the first time, was a tall, slender, frail-looking young woman, her face rather too long and square-jawed to be actually pretty, but attractive all the same, and with beautiful, deep-blue eyes. Her name was Marguerite LeHand. Everyone called her Missy, and everyone loved her for her gaiety, her gentle kindness, her unfailing sweetness of temper, qualities joined in uncommon linkage with a clear-eyed and wholly unsentimental realism, a remarkable astuteness—particularly in her judgments of people—and with the efficient arts and industry of a topflight secretary. During the 1920 vice-presidential campaign, when Eleanor had

17

first met her, she had been the secretary of Roosevelt's campaign manager. After the campaign, Eleanor had asked her to come to Hyde Park for a few weeks to help her husband deal with a great pile of correspondence that had accumulated on his desk. She had remained with the Roosevelts ever since as Franklin's personal secretary and, especially during and immediately after the polio crisis, had become much more than an employee, more even than a close family friend. To all intents and purposes she was an actual member of the family.

To dine at the Roosevelt table, which was almost always a crowded one, was to nourish one's mind and spirit along with one's body. The talk was invariably abundant, spirited, flavorful. Everyone was encouraged to speak his or her mind. Arguments were frequent, and on occasion, heated.

During a Saturday night dinner, on a later weekend with the Roosevelts, Marion found herself talking about a tour she had recently made of the West Virginia and Pennsylvania coal fields, where the miners were on strike. She did so at considerable length (". . . I was so full of what I had been through that it was hard to talk about anything else," she remembers) and in terms sympathetic to the strikers, condemnatory of the absentee mine owners. When she spoke of the Vittondale Mine, where the measures taken against "outside agitators" were especially harsh, she suddenly became aware that all other talk had ceased. Nor was there any response to her words. She was a little embarrassed, "but I thought they were just getting bored."

It was the custom at Hyde Park to gather in the library after dinner. When the gathering there broke up that evening, and Marion went over to Franklin to say good night, he asked her to stay a bit, if she were not "too awfully tired," and talk to him alone. He wanted to have her tell him more about her coal field experience; but, he begged, less "emotionally" ("I know you're very emotional," he said, smiling) and more "realistically." Especially was he interested in what she had to say about the Vittondale Mine.

"Did you know that that is a Delano mine?" he asked.

Her face flushed as she shook her head, rather miserably. She

18

understood, now, that sudden silence at table and why Granny, especially, "had been a little cool" to her afterward.

But Roosevelt at once put her at ease. He told her that "Uncle Fred," his mother's younger brother, was in charge of the Delano mining properties. He would phone Uncle Fred, he said, and ask him to come over to talk with both of them. And he did so next day.

"You know, Uncle Fred," said Roosevelt, as Marion remembers it, "as long as these conditions exist, my family does not want any income from that mine. And I'll appreciate your seeing to it."

Frederick Delano, evidently in full agreement, said he'd go down to Vittondale as soon as he possibly could—and the mine was not mentioned again.

Marion was relieved, that Sunday morning, when Granny greeted her with affectionate warmth, her "coldness" having departed during the night. And when Granny said good-bye that afternoon, her "Come again" was no mere formality but an expressed recognition of the inevitable. Nancy and Marion would indeed come again, and again. They were being accepted into the small, close-knit Roosevelt inner circle, the most intimate of family circles, of which the only member Marion had not yet met was Louis Howe—and only in retrospect would this quick acceptance seem to Marion strange and wonderful; at the time it seemed perfectly natural, as everything about the Roosevelts seemed always natural, never artificial or pretentious.

A few days later she did meet Louis Howe. She was introduced to him by Eleanor in the Roosevelts' New York City house.

At first sight he struck her as one of the ugliest men she had ever seen. She had to look down upon him, and quite far down, for he was barely five feet tall, and the upturned face she saw was the wizened face of an old man, though he was only fifty-one. His leathery facial skin appeared unclean—an effect produced, as Marion later learned, by the innumerable tiny scars of a boyhood bicycle accident, wherein he had been pitched hard, face down, upon a graveled road. He was obviously sickly. His forehead had permanent frown creases above the nose, as if plucked together by chronic pain; dark pouches were under his eyes; and his cheeks were deeply hollowed. His head appeared abnormally large, but this was only because it perched precariously, or so it seemed, atop an incredibly scrawny neck, which he endeavored to hide behind a high, starched collar—a neck that was in turn upthrust from a narrow, emaciated body upon which his clothes hung loosely. There were vague stains on his shirt and tie, and flakes and streaks of cigarette ash were on his coat. Later she would know that he consumed three or four packs of Sweet Caporals a day, and seldom bothered to take the one he was smoking from his mouth. He moved, he breathed, he had his being amid a cloud of smoke and drifting ash.

This last was one of the things about him that Granny simply could not stand. Indeed, there was nothing about him that pleased Sara Delano Roosevelt, and for all her good manners, she made small effort to hide her dislike of him—and on his part he made small effort to avoid giving offense to such as Granny. Eleanor herself confessed she had found the little man repulsive when first he joined forces with her husband in 1912, and for years thereafter. "The fact that he had rather extraordinary eyes and a fine mind I was fool enough not to have discovered yet," she later wrote, "and it was by externals alone that I judged him. . . ." Not until the 1920 vice-presidential campaign, when he put himself out to make her feel herself a vital part of what was going on, had she got to know him well enough to begin to like him; and not until the two of them labored side by side during the darkest days of Roosevelt's polio crisis had they become fast friends.

Of course, Eleanor had prepared Marion somewhat for this introduction. Marion was therefore not as put off as she might otherwise have been by his physical appearance and brusque manner. She looked into soft, brown eyes that were indeed "extraordinary" in that there shone out of them an unexpected aesthetic sensitivity (he wrote verse, he painted watercolors, she would learn) and an even less expected warmth and kindliness, along with a sharp, quick intelligence, joined to a rather mordant wit. She decided that she, too, liked him, and that the two of them would become, as in the event they did become, fast friends.

20

T W O

FROM THIS TIME FORWARD, Nancy, Marion, and Eleanor Roosevelt were a threesome whose motto might well have been that of Dumas' Three Musketeers—especially insofar as they fought side by side against a common foe in perennial political warfare. They were inseparable, too, on other matters. They loved one another—no one can read the letters they wrote to each other when apart without being impressed by the warmth and depth of their mutual affection. They counted upon one another, helped one another, shared experiences, took unfailing joy in each other's company, and trusted one another absolutely. When together they built a cottage— Val Kill Cottage—on Roosevelt acres, several items of its furnishing bore the initials of all three of them, E.M.N. Several of the products of Eleanor's constant and, it would seem, compulsive employment of her knitting needles did so as well—the covers she made for bureaus and dressing tables—and so did some of the silver. Gradually, as time passed, each came to know many of the others' vital secrets and—Eleanor especially—confided in the others some of her most intimate troubles and concerns.

There were psychic dangers here, obvious to an outside observer: the excessive closeness of the relationship seemed certain to breed a mutual possessiveness against which one or more of them, since each was an intrinsically strong individual with a large growth potential, must sooner or later rebel. One would have expected this to happen within three or four years. The fact that it didn't, that instead the relationship continued unimpaired for half a generation, testifies to its unusual nature, which in turn testifies to the rare personal qualities of its participants.

For all their intimacy, each kept a part of herself apart, isolate, and was careful not to invade the privacies nor breach the walls of reticence the others wished or were compelled to maintain. Each had special abilities and circumstantial assets that the others lacked; each took a sincere pride in talents possessed by the others but lacking in herself; and these special abilities, assets, talents, though often if not generally pooled among them as a resource upon which all might draw, were also always recognized as distinct individual contributions to their common weal. Fifteen years later, in *This Is My Story*, Eleanor wrote: "Miss Cook and Miss Dickerman and I . . . had been first drawn together through the work which we were doing together. This is, I think, one of the most satisfactory ways of making and keeping friends."

They were certainly tremendously busy always, all three of them, and they interested one another conversationally when they did not actively involve one another in their quite widely various activities. During the summer Marion had accepted employment as teacher in the small, expensive, highly prestigious Todhunter School for Girls in New York; she began her work there a week or so after her second weekend at Hyde Park. The Todhunter balance of discipline and spontaneity, of uniformity (the girls wore uniforms) and individuality—reflecting the

personality of its owner, Miss Winifred Todhunter, an Englishwoman
—accorded almost precisely with Marion's natural predilections. She
spoke of this enthusiastically to Eleanor, who was at once interested to
the extent of wondering if she herself might not actively teach some
day. At the moment, however, she and Nancy were absorbed by the
"women's side" of New York's gubernatorial campaign. Eleanor was a
delegate from Dutchess County (Hyde Park is a part of it) to the State
Convention in Syracuse, where Al Smith was "nominated with great
enthusiasm," as Louis Howe telegraphed FDR, and where she and
Henry Morgenthau, Jr., of Hopewell Junction, with whom and with
whose wife Elinor the Roosevelts were then just beginning to be close
friends, "led the Dutchess County delegation with the banner three
times around the hall." Subsequently, helped by Marion's and Nancy's
experienced advice, along with FDR's and Howe's, Eleanor worked
hard for Smith in overwhelmingly Republican Dutchess, which that
year was carried by the Republican candidate Nathan Miller by a bare
1,000 votes. Al Smith won the election by a comfortable majority, a
victory for greater participation and effectiveness of women in politics
in view of the fact that Smith, though he was certainly no feminist,
was inclined to favor such activity, whereas conservative Miller had
opposed it.

Marion and Nancy were members of the Women's Trade Union
League, which Eleanor now joined, the three of them working with the
director of the New York branch, Rose Schneiderman, and with Maud
Swartz on a variety of projects for women workers in, chiefly, New
York City's garment industry. Nancy and Eleanor especially worked
politically for Trade Union League legislative objectives—for laws
abolishing child labor, establishing a minimum wage, and limiting the
work week for women to forty-eight hours. When it was later decided
that WTUL must have an enlarged headquarters, in a five-story
brownstone on Lexington Avenue, it was Eleanor who chaired the
highly successful fund-raising committee; and when evening classes
for women workers began there, it was Marion and Eleanor who
helped make the project go, Eleanor reading to the girls one night a

week (she loved to read aloud), while Marion conducted a class in literature. By then both Rose and Maud were frequent guests at the Roosevelts' Sixty-fifth Street home and at Hyde Park. But for a long time Eleanor hesitated to introduce them to Granny on Granny's home ground (the Hyde Park mansion was Granny's personal property) because she was uncertain of their welcome, they being so clearly and emphatically "lower class" in background and accent (red-haired Rose was an immigrant from Russian Poland and Maud was of England's proletariat). Eleanor confessed as much to Marion, who came later to believe that her friend was inclined to worry overmuch about such things, underrating Granny's social grace and sensitivity. (Once, at dinner in Hyde Park, as Marion vividly remembers, "a certain gentleman was sitting at her [Granny's] right, and fingerbowls were placed in front of us, and then, when ice cream was passed, this gentleman put his ice cream in his fingerbowl. When the ice cream came to Granny she put hers in the fingerbowl while continuing her conversation uninterrupted.")

Eleanor, Marion, and Nancy were active in the League of Women Voters, of which Eleanor had become a New York State board member by the time Marion first met her. Her assignment was to report on legislative proposals that the LWV might wish to support and on the fate in Washington and Albany of the legislation to which the league was committed. She had accepted this assignment only after being assured of expert professional help. This last was provided by Elizabeth F. Read, who was actively engaged in law practice and who became Eleanor's personal lawyer as well as her lifelong friend. Quietly but immensely competent in all that she undertook, Elizabeth tempered her idealistic commitments with hard common sense. Through Elizabeth, Eleanor made friends with Esther Lape, who was also on the LWV state board. Esther shared a Greenwich Village apartment with Elizabeth, and coedited with her a weekly legislative review, published by the league, entitled *City-State-Nation*. With trained skills as a publicist, Esther was somewhat more outgoing and manifestly brilliant than Elizabeth, if also somewhat less hardheaded.

When, in the summer of 1923, Edward M. Bok, former publisher and editor of the *Ladies Home Journal*, offered a prize of $100,000 for "the best practicable plan by which the U.S. may cooperate with other nations to achieve and preserve the peace of the world," it was Esther Lape, with Eleanor as a principal assistant, who became the director of the hugely publicized contest.* Inevitably, Eleanor's friends became Marion's also, and Nancy's. The reverse was also true. It was largely through Marion and Nancy that Eleanor formed her warm friendship with Caroline O'Day.

Even among the group of remarkable women with whom the three-some of Eleanor-Marion-Nancy was now involved, Mrs. O'Day was outstanding. Born Caroline Love Goodwin shortly after the Civil War on a plantation near Perry, Georgia, she was raised in the southern aristocracy but was definitely not *of* that aristocracy in her strikingly liberal social and political views. One would hardly have expected her wealthy husband, Daniel O'Day, a vice-president of Standard Oil, to share these views, yet he seems to have done so. At least "he was an enthusiastic advocate of women's suffrage," according to Marion, "and it was he who suggested that Mrs. O'Day march in the first great suf-frage parade." It is not recorded whether he was "a dedicated pacifist," as his wife emphatically was when he died in 1916. Thereafter, while devoting herself to her three children, she devoted herself also, more actively than before, to the suffrage and pacifist movements, continuing to hold pacifist meetings in her home in Rye after the United States had entered the First World War. When agents of the Department of Justice were posted at the entrance of her estate, as they were from the spring of 1917 until after the Armistice, for the purpose of listing "the names of all persons attending her meetings for peace," she refreshed

---

* More than 22,000 "peace plans" were submitted; and after the winner was announced, in January 1924, the contest's conception and execution, with particular emphasis upon the fact that it was directed by an all-female policy committee, became the object of virulent isolationist attack in the Senate and of a Senate investigation designed to prove—though it wholly failed to prove —that the contest had been rigged.

them daily with hot coffee in the cold months and lemonade in the warm ones, carried down to them by her household staff.

Amid the reversal of mood, the embittered disillusionment that quickly followed the Armistice, Caroline O'Day's wartime stand made her a heroine to many who had angrily condemned her in 1918. She continued to be extremely active in Democratic political organization; and this led to her becoming, in 1923, associate chairman of the Democratic State Committee and also the head of the Women's Division. Nancy Cook continued as executive secretary—that is, the actual administrator.

Thereafter, for many years, Caroline O'Day was but slightly less close to Eleanor, Nancy, and Marion than these three were to each other. She had no great physical beauty, but her blue-eyed gaze was as kindly and compassionate as it was sharply, penetratingly intelligent. One sensed that the workings of her iron moral commitments would be relatively frictionless, being lubricated by a warmly flowing sense of humor, and that she would be a good companion, could even be great fun, on active expeditions.

And so she proved to be, on spring weekends and through the early summer of 1923. Sometimes with Nancy, sometimes with Marion or Eleanor, occasionally with all three of them, she set out upon energetic tours of the upstate counties, giving talks to groups of people, discussing local situations with local politicos, recruiting women members for the party, and struggling to establish truly viable local upstate Democratic organizations. A prevailing prejudice among rural women was that the Republican party was the party of successful people, of social prestige; that the Democratic party was a collection of Catholics, first- and second-generation immigrants, urban workers of the lowest class, and ne'er-do-wells. Of this prejudice these four women were living contradictions; they could reduce it by sheer personal example, being themselves obviously cultivated, socially prestigious, professionally competent.

And in general their upstate enterprise succeeded to a greater and politically more important degree than seems to have been realized by city-born and -bred Al Smith, who in those years openly aspired to the Presidency. Al Smith continued always to write off rural and small-town New York as hopelessly Republican. But Franklin Roosevelt did not. Louis Howe did not. They were convinced that the good health of the party, and the prosperity of their personal political ambition, required a strong upstate organization to counteract and overbalance the New York City machine. Hence these two paid great attention to all that Eleanor and her close friends were doing politically, and encouraged their doing of it. They advised. They made suggestions. They even—Howe in particular—initiated projects for them.

Louis Howe coached Eleanor in public speaking. Marion remembers how he would sit in the back of a room where Eleanor was speaking, then tell her afterward, often with a harsh frankness that caused her face to flush, what was right and wrong about her performance. He was competent to do so, because from his early boyhood he had been intensely interested in the stage, and in Saratoga Springs, New York, where he grew up, he had been a most active member of amateur theatrical groups—had acted, designed and built scenery, even written comedies. He had an excellent speaking voice; he knew how to handle himself on stage, how to project. He helped Eleanor to overcome her tendency to giggle and pitch her voice too high when self-conscious, as she always was, in those early days, before a crowd.

It was also at Louis Howe's suggestion, and with his active behind-the-scenes help—he having been a newspaperman for twenty-odd years before joining forces with FDR—that a mimeographed, haphazardly produced "news bulletin" of the Women's Division was transformed by Eleanor, Marion, and Nancy into a professionally edited and printed publication, the *Women's Democratic News*, whose monthly dozen pages contained articles by prominent Democrats, news and analyses of legislative proposals, reports from women's county organizations, and enough advertising (solicited by Eleanor, for the most part) to pay the printing costs. The first issue appeared in May 1925, and listed as both editor and treasurer Mrs. Franklin D. Roosevelt; as business manager, Nancy Cook; as secretary, Marion Dickerman; and, as president and vice-president respectively of the publishing corporation, Mrs. Daniel O'Day and Mrs. Henry Morgenthau, Jr.

By then—indeed, as early as the summer of 1923—there was a more than dim awareness by Marion and Nancy that their work with Eleanor for Al Smith's advancement and the strengthening of the New York Democratic party had a further, a transcendent end. It was an end that in 1923 and early 1924 seemed remote and problematical to Marion; toward it Eleanor's personal inward attitude, as she revealed this to Marion and Nancy, was curiously mixed, increasingly ambivalent, ambiguous; and it might easily have been lost sight of altogether—even FDR seemed sometimes inclined to forget or ignore it—had not Louis Howe kept fixed upon it a gaze of burning intensity that never wavered, and committed to it an energy of purpose that was amazing in a man so frail and rickety of body and so often totally incapacitated by illness. His was the vision and voice and arm of destiny in this regard. And as the months passed into years, his sense of destiny was infused into all in the innermost circle. What they were doing—the ultimate aim of all their effort in politics—was making Franklin D. Roosevelt President of the United States.

This transcendent end imparted to the friendship of the three women —giving to everything they did together, even to things evidently wholly unrelated to politics, even to things purely familial and personal—an excitement it would not otherwise have had, along with an extra dimension of significance. A historical dimension. They intermittently saw and pervasively felt themselves actors in, as well as spectators of, a grand historical drama already written and awaiting only their performance of it. Hence the homeliest gesture, the most trivial happening acquired a symbolic meaning; it was not merely itself alone, it was also an element of some tremendous whole and a sign, a portent, of other elements of that whole.

Yet this sense of history resulted in not the slightest lessening of spontaneity, risk, shock, surprise, suspense in their daily lives. If it was inevitable that Franklin Roosevelt become President of the United States, as Louis Howe—and he himself—believed, it was identically inevitable that he face grave hazards and overcome stubborn obstacles through the most adroit maneuvering and strenuous effort on his way to the White House, including the hazards and obstacles of self-doubt, of temporary (though sometimes prolonged) lapses of faith and confidence. Thus with his polio affliction. It was Roosevelt's conviction, never openly explicitly avowed by him, but felt by all of the innermost circle, that his polio was a "trial by fire," as Eleanor called it, imposed by God for the purpose of testing and purifying him. The fierce physical agony he had suffered, the dark nights of utter despair through which he had passed, the incredibly harsh regimen he now imposed upon himself as he struggled to walk again—all were designed to prepare him for the great historical tasks that must ultimately be his.

In early 1923 Roosevelt rented a houseboat, the *Weona II*, for cruising in Florida waters, and spent weeks upon it—fishing, sunning himself, and exercising on its deck—with great benefit to his overall health and some slight strengthening of his withered legs. He then, in partnership with a friend, John S. Lawrence, bought a houseboat that he christened *Larooco* (a contraction of Lawrence, Roosevelt, and Co.) and lived upon it in Florida waters in early 1924. Eleanor did not accompany him on these expeditions. She, Nancy, and Marion were very much involved, however, at least emotionally, in the enterprise upon which FDR embarked soon after his return from Florida to 49 East Sixty-fifth Street in the spring of 1924.

Al Smith was preparing that spring to make a major bid for the Democratic presidential nomination by the party's national convention, which was to meet in late June in New York City's Madison Square Garden. Roosevelt had agreed to make the speech placing Smith in nomination, thereby committing himself to an effort more physical than mental. Although he seems to have drafted a nominating speech (dictated to Missy) at Hyde Park, the one he was actually to give was written by Al Smith's close friend and associate, Judge Joseph M. Proskauer. (As a matter of fact, FDR raised strong initial objections to what was destined to be his address's most famous passage, derived from William Wordsworth ["This is the Happy Warrior, this is he/ Whom every man in arms should wish to be"], whereby Al Smith was identified for his contemporaries, and for the history books, as the Happy Warrior.) His overriding concern was to transport himself physically, unaided, without falling down, from his seat at the rear of the convention platform to the podium. At that time he had to do so on crutches: his steel-braced legs were not yet strong enough to permit that semblance of walking which, with the aid of a supporting arm, characterized his later public appearances, and he had to make sure that the podium itself would sustain his full leaning weight, for only by gripping its sides could he hold himself upright. "Nobody knows how that man worked," says Marion, who was a witness to his effort. "They measured off in the library of the Sixty-fifth Street house just the distance to the podium, and he practiced getting across that distance. Oh, he struggled."

And he triumphed!

Marion vividly remembers the triumph, which she witnessed with Eleanor and Nancy and Granny from a gallery seat. It was soon after the day's session opened, on a morning hot, humid, overcast. The crowd as it gathered was rather dull, listless. But the hall was electrified by the sight of Roosevelt making his way, on cue, across the stage, slowly, concentratedly, with a tense awareness of risk that communicated itself to all who watched. Marion held her breath and prayed.

It seemed a long hour before he reached the podium. Bracing himself against the stand, gripping the lectern with both hands, he drew himself upright and lifted high his head, smiling a rather remote smile, withdrawn, as if he smiled to himself amid the thunderous applause and cheers. At that instant, destiny chose to bless him visibly, radiantly. Dark clouds parted above the Garden's roof, and through the skylight came a burst of sunlight. Roosevelt's lifted head was spotlighted by it ("—you know what a handsome person he was," says Marion); and the crowd's enthusiastic reception became tinged with awe.

30

There was not the slightest diminution of dramatic excitement during the nominating address that followed.

Marion had never heard Franklin Roosevelt in public speech before. She thrilled—she felt the thousands around her thrilling—to a rich tenor voice that, with a perfect timing of pauses and emphases, almost sang the eloquent phrases. Judge Proskauer's speech, designed to appeal as much to the heads as to the hearts of the audience, became in Roosevelt's presentation of it a primarily emotional experience. And when at last he sang out the closing words, the Wordsworth lines joined to the name of Alfred E. Smith, "the crowd just went crazy," says Marion. "Oh, it was stupendous, really stupendous!"

That night, Eleanor Roosevelt and Caroline O'Day were twin hostesses at a reception in the Sixty-fifth Street house for New York's delegates to the convention. Marion went up a little early from the Greenwich Village apartment on West Twelfth Street, where she and Nancy now lived, "to see if I could be of any help." But she had barely spoken to Eleanor and Caroline when the Roosevelt butler came up to her. Mr. Roosevelt was in his room upstairs, the butler said, and wanted her to come up to him. She went at once.

He was sitting upright in his bed. Obviously he was very tired, but the face he turned toward her as she entered was alight. He held out his arms to her.

"Marion," he said, "I *did* it!"

As it turned out, the morning light that had shone upon Roosevelt was the only bright spot amid the murky gloom of the most disastrous political convention since that of the Democrats in 1860. Balloting on presidential nominees continued through more than a hundred roll-call votes of the states, its only effect a widening of the breach between the partisans of Al Smith and those of William Gibbs McAdoo, until finally an exhausted, totally dispirited convention turned to a dark horse, a wealthy corporation lawyer named John W. Davis, whose basic economic and political views were virtually indistinguishable from those of his Republican opponent, Calvin Coolidge.

The ensuing presidential campaign was, for the Democrats, an exercise in futility, and FDR took virtually no part in it. The great Teapot Dome scandal had splattered crude oil all over the Republican party's national organization, but none of it seemed to stick, in the electorate's view, to the person of Calvin Coolidge. The scandal was Harding's responsibility, and Harding was dead. Moreover, a principal villain of the scandal, oilman Edward L. Doheny, was a prominent Democrat. Finally, Davis, with his big business commitments, was in no position, even if he had the desire, to develop the issue of big business domination of government. It remained for a third candidate, Wisconsin's Senator Robert M. La Follette, to develop this issue through a third party, the national Progressive party, which he temporarily revived that year and whose presidential candidate he became.

Nor was Davis a personally inspiring figure. He was entertained by the Roosevelts at Hyde Park in the second week of August. Marion, a house guest there at the time, along with Caroline O'Day and Nancy, liked the candidate personally ("he was a fine man") but she could develop no enthusiasm over him. "He didn't arouse great loyalty." He aroused no loyalty at all in the head of the Women's Division of the New York Democratic party. That evening in Hyde Park, Caroline O'Day disappeared from the house for hours. "Where on earth have you been?" Marion asked her upon her return. Caroline looked a bit sheepish, but defiant. She had gone to a La Follette meeting, she said—"and you know, when they passed the hat, I emptied my purse!"

But Caroline joined with Eleanor, Marion, and Nancy in enthusiastic, active support of the candidacy of Al Smith for reelection as Governor of New York that fall—and this despite the fact that Eleanor's first cousin, Theodore Roosevelt, Jr., was Smith's Republican opponent. The four women joined happily in what Eleanor later admitted was a "rough stunt" (Marion thought so, too) designed by Louis Howe to remind New York's electorate that TR, Jr., had been Harding's Assistant Secretary of the Navy at the time the naval oil reserves were secretly and illegally transferred to the Department of the Interior and then fraudulently leased to private drillers. Howe's design was a brown papier-mâché "teapot" that could be fitted over an automobile's body and whose spout emitted actual steam. The Teapot Dome float, in Eleanor's later words, "led the procession of cars which toured the state, following the Republican [gubernatorial] candidate . . . wherever he went."

On November 4 Al Smith was reelected with a majority of 140,000 votes—a tremendous victory for him, in view of the fact that Calvin Coolidge carried New York by 700,000 and defeated Davis nationally by 16 million to 8 million, with La Follette winning nearly 5 million. Two women governors were elected—the first in the nation's history.

THREE

I T I S Marion's belief that the decision to build the cottage was made in the fall of 1924. She vividly remembers a golden Saturday afternoon when FDR, Eleanor, Nan, and she, with young John and Franklin, Jr. (everyone called him "Brother" or "Brud"; Anna was "Sister"), were picnicking together at their favorite picnic spot on the Hyde Park acres. It was beside a placid stream, named Val Kill by the seventeenth-century Dutch, which still ran sparkling clear in the early 1920s through an open, empty landscape of wood and meadow, its appearance little changed since the Dutch first settled there. The picnic was a typically exuberant Roosevelt one, with much talk and laughter and great quantities of food. Everyone had a grand time—and as evening shadows began to fall, Eleanor remarked rather wistfully that this must be their last picnic, their last weekend in Hyde Park that year.

34

"Why do you say that?" asked FDR.

"Because, as you know, Granny is closing the house for the winter."

He looked at her and then, thoughtfully, at the brook, the meadow, the wooded slopes. A truly lovely spot.

"But aren't you girls silly?" he said at last. "This isn't Mother's land. I bought this acreage myself. And why shouldn't you three have a cottage here of your own, so you could come and go as you please? Or—" he turned to Nan and Marion—"you might actually make this your country house. If you'll mark out the land you want, I'll give you a life interest in it, with the understanding that it reverts to my estate upon the death of the last survivor."

Soon thereafter a formal legal document was drawn up, "signed by all parties and witnessed by Louis Howe," effecting the arrangement FDR had suggested. During the following winter months, Eleanor, Marion, and Nancy spent much pleasant time talking over plans, and Nan made a small model of the proposed cottage that embodied their agreed ideas.

Thus Marion's recollection.

But living memory plays tricks with the order of events. The legal document in Marion's possession, wherein FDR gave a life lease to "a portion of the so-called Bennett Farm" to Nancy Cook, Marion Dickerman, and Anna E. Roosevelt, was drawn up, not in late 1924, but on January 29, 1926, by which time the project it sanctioned was virtually completed. Moreover, on August 5, 1924—which was many weeks before the first suggestion for the cottage was made, according to Marion's remembrance—FDR seemingly referred to the project in a letter to a contractor friend of his, Elliott Brown, with whom he had made tentative plans for construction of a swimming pool a few yards from the Hyde Park mansion. He wrote: "My missus and some of her female political friends want to build a shack on a stream in the back woods [Val Kill was a mile and a half from the house] and want, instead of a beautiful marble bath, to have the stream dug out so as to form an old-fashioned swimming hole." He indicated that he approved the idea.

35

Certainly, by the fall of 1923, the happy intimacy of the threefold friendship, and the conviction of its permanence (none of the three believed it could ever fail), had been firmly established and tested by experience—sufficiently so to justify the lifetime arrangement that was in fact made.

The three had shared a long moment of terror in 1922 when young Franklin (Brother) slipped into water over his head in Granny's ice pond—that is, the pond from which ice was cut in the winter for storage in the icehouse. Unable to swim, he had been rescued by the three women, none of whom could swim either, only with great difficulty and good luck. FDR, told of the episode, issued an order: "You three girls are going to learn to swim!" And so they did, or tried to do, during the following winter. They all went to YWCA swimming classes, where Marion learned to swim fairly well and Eleanor indifferently well. Nancy, alas, learned not at all. (For all her phenomenal manual dexterity she was the opposite of athletic.) In the late spring of 1923 Eleanor and Marion set out to teach Brother and John to swim but, says Marion, "the boys were soon far ahead of us."

Marion and Nancy had shared, too, in Eleanor's determined efforts to avoid the child-rearing mistakes she felt had been made in the case of her three eldest children. These eldest had largely been raised by a succession of English governesses chosen by Granny, all of whom were excessively authoritarian and one or two of whom were actively sadistic. Yet at the same time Granny herself had been permissive of behavior her grandchildren's parents sought to forbid—had been lavish in her gifts to them, including gifts of things she knew Eleanor or Franklin had specifically denied them—with the result that parental authority was subverted. Alternatively and confusingly overdisciplined and overindulged, Anna, James, and Elliott, each strong-willed and tremendously energetic, had grown into adolescence without adequately firm outer guidelines and, almost certainly, without properly developed self-controls, either.

The case of Elliott appeared particularly unfortunate.

His had been a deeply troubled childhood. He had been a sickly infant, had been forced to wear steel braces on bowed legs, had suffered a succession of ailments and painful accidents; and these physical woes had been joined to psychic ones. Of a sullen, rebellious disposition, with a flaming temper and a deep-seated conviction that the world was against him, he reacted to real or fancied wrongs in aggressive ways that were harmful to himself and sometimes dangerously cruel to others. He displayed a particularly ugly mood when, aged twelve in September 1922, he was forced to enter Groton, the exclusive Massachusetts boys' school his father had attended and where James was happily enrolled in the third form. Marion was immediately informed of the scenes he then made, and learned, too, that Eleanor not only sympathized with her son in this instance, being convinced that a lad of twelve was too young to be removed from the parental roof, but also sympathized with him in general, being convinced that his troubles were to a considerable degree her fault. Almost simultaneously with his conception had occurred the death at the age of eight months of her third-born child, "the biggest and most beautiful of all the babies—the first baby Franklin," as she wrote twenty-seven years later. All through the months of her pregnancy with Elliott she had been morbidly depressed (". . . I made myself and all those around me most unhappy . . ."), and ever after she believed that this unhappiness had been communicated to the new life she carried in her womb. *She* was to blame! And Marion—Anna, too, in later years—became aware of how Elliott, who (significantly) bore the name of Eleanor's beloved father, sensed and learned to play upon this feeling of guilt his mother had, learned to use it to get his way with her.

"Elliott could twist her around his finger," says Marion.

When Marion first met her, Eleanor had long since ceased to permit Granny to choose the governesses: she chose them herself. She herself spent much more time with the younger children than she had with the older, and in this maternal enterprise she involved her two bosom friends. The three women took the two boys on expeditions to the Statue of Liberty and other points of interest in and around New York

City. They picnicked with them on weekends at Hyde Park. They all went on a long camping trip one summer, making use of the Roosevelt's seven-passenger Buick, of which every seat was filled, since they also had with them two other young boys—George Draper, Jr., the son of FDR's doctor, and Henry Roosevelt, the son of Eleanor's younger brother, Hall.

The seven had with them a tent for the three adults, a pup tent for the boys, a stove (Nancy Cook was cook), and they lived across the green summer land a rootless gypsy existence for days on end, pitching their tents at night in whatever spot of wood or field struck their fancy. Theirs was no random wandering, however. They had a planned itinerary as they drove northward along the Hudson, Lake George, Lake Champlain—they stopped at Fort Ticonderoga, they stopped at Ausable Chasm—and on into Canada, pausing briefly in Montreal and for a couple of days in Quebec, where they reveled in hotel luxuries after their rough life in the open air. There were excitements, anxieties. Brother gashed his leg with a hatchet, and since Eleanor, having administered first aid, did not take him to a doctor to have the cut sewn up, it took weeks to heal. Seven-year-old George Draper and John, without telling anyone, left the hotel in Quebec and wandered alone through the streets, returning to report calmly to three frantic adults that they had simply gone sight-seeing—which, after all, was what they had all come to do. Then the party came down through the White Mountains of New Hampshire, and across Maine to Campobello Island.

At Campobello they lived for two weeks in the Roosevelt "cottage" of some thirty-four rooms, where FDR had suffered his polio attack precisely two years before and which Eleanor had not seen since then. Nancy and Marion had never seen it before. They soon felt, however, as if they had long known the summer island life as the Roosevelts lived it, for Eleanor talked at length and frankly about how it had been in the past, and gave them photographs of that past. It was almost as if they could remember seeing a lithe and vigorous FDR run in a swim-suit on strong handsome legs down the slope to the shore and plunge into the little swimming pool of trapped tidal water he had constructed there (it employed an ingenious floodgate arrangement) before hoisting sail on the *Vireo*, the Roosevelt's twenty-four-foot gaff-rigged keel sloop. FDR had sailed her for long strenuous hours on the day polio first struck him. And Marion even felt as if she had been in this house during that grim crisis, when all was hushed here, and tense—when what radiated from FDR was not vital light and warmth and gaiety but dark pain and terror and death, he lying utterly paralyzed in a second-floor bedroom, the fever beating through his blood, while Eleanor and Louis Howe struggled desperately day and night to cope with an illness whose very name was unknown to them but whose fatal seriousness was only too obvious. For Eleanor spoke of this, too, in matter-of-fact detail, yet in a way that conveyed emotion.

Surely one could understand and sympathize if at that juncture, and through the long grinding ordeal that followed, Eleanor was hardened, and had hardened herself, in ways conducive of duty and work performance but inhibitory of any natural, relaxed playfulness. Her playful tendencies, she admitted to her friends, had been limited and restrained to begin with. From early childhood she had been excessively conscientious and inclined toward puritan austerities—inclined to associate ease and beauty with sin, difficulty and plainness with virtue, while on another plane she envied easiness and admired (with some envy) the beautiful. But the ordeal of her husband's polio certainly further confirmed her in such attitudes emotionally, and this at a time when, intellectually, she most seriously doubted the validity of puritanism, doubted even that she was truly a Christian in her deepest belief. The irony, adding nothing to her peace of mind and soul, stemmed largely from a profound psychic hurt of which Marion and Nancy did not then precisely know, though Eleanor had given hints of it on several occasions. Fortunately she had a sense of humor; it enabled her to retain balance and perspective, and to use experience for spiritual growth. It enabled her, often, to make a species of play out of the work she did. But at the same time, in those years, her essential earnestness almost always caused her to make a species of work out of play, for she could never feel, deep down, that play could ever be its own justification and end; it must be always and only a respite from serious concerns, if perhaps necessary for a renewal of the self for the labors that *were* important.

All of which made it difficult for her to establish with her children the wholly happy companionship, the easy rapport, for which she yearned. The camping trip was part of her deliberate effort to "substitute for Father" by doing with the youngest boys what their father would have done had he not been crippled. But it was almost impossible for her to do this. Her femininity in a male-oriented society militated against her acceptance by young boys in what they persisted in regarding as a masculine role. Moreover, she tried too hard: there grew in the boys a suspicion, confessed to their sister Anna, that their mother might not *really* love them, but was only doing her duty by them—a suspicion encouraged by the fact that she must (she felt) often counteract with a nay-saying discipline Granny's overindulgences of them and, to some extent, her husband's. So it often happened on this trip that three of the boys—Franklin, John, and George—seemed to draw together in common cause, raising against their elders bland walls of reserve behind which, as Marion sensed, they lived secret lives.

As for the fourth boy, Eleanor's nephew Henry Roosevelt, he was the outsider—unhappy, tense, withdrawn. There was something lost and jangled about him, a deficiency of self-control, as there was in so many of the Oyster Bay (Theodore Roosevelt) branch of the Roosevelt family to which Eleanor herself belonged (her father Elliott was TR's younger brother)—and Eleanor's attempts to force or persuade the other three to include this boy in their activities served but to emphasize their essential rejection of him. This cast a pall—a thin one; the sunlight did shine through—upon a generally joyous expedition, and was particularly distressing to Eleanor because she then worried so much (she would worry far more in the years ahead) about the boy's father, her younger brother Hall, with whom her relationship had been almost maternal as he grew up and who was now extremely "impa-

40

tient, at times ruthless" but "quicker than anyone I had ever known and with a brilliant mind," as she later wrote. He had just divorced his first wife, the mother of three of his children, the youngest named after her, and it was in the hope of assuaging the traumatic pain this home-breaking had inflicted on Henry that Eleanor had arranged for him to come on the trip. The effect, alas, was opposite.

One Sunday morning on Campobello, while Eleanor, Marion, and Nancy attended church services, John and George took one of the Roosevelt rowboats and in it rowed across Passamaquoddy Bay. This was strictly forbidden; the waters of Passamaquoddy are extremely treacherous. When the boys returned just before lunch, a frightened, furious Eleanor lectured them and ordered John to go to his room and stay there until further notice. "I can't punish you," she said to George, "because you're not my son—but if you feel you deserve the same punishment as John you may go to your room." To her helpless surprise and humiliation, he merely smiled, shook his head, and said he really thought he wouldn't. The rowing had made him hungry. He joined the others at luncheon, and during it "tried to exert all his charm," as Marion remembers—"and he was one of the most charming young boys that I have ever known."

Rose Schneiderman, who had arrived as house guest, was present at this "very troubled" luncheon. Her vivid, redheaded sense of justice was outraged.

"That boy simply must not be allowed to get away with this," she said to Marion after luncheon, "and Mrs. Roosevelt can do nothing more. Can you?"

So Marion asked George to take a walk with her, during which she "made up an apocryphal story, which I told him, laid in Greece, which seemed quite a safe distance away." He listened with increasing thoughtfulness. Upon their return to the house he said he guessed he had better go to his room after all—and he did.

On the Roosevelt motor launch a couple of days later, with Captain Calder (he had charge of the Roosevelt boats) at the helm, Marion, who was an excellent storyteller, was urged by the boys to tell them another story; she hesitated, looking directly at George as she did so. He smiled a rueful smile. "Yes," he said, "*do* tell us a story—but don't have it about the Greeks!"

In the chill of the evenings on Campobello, after the boys had gone to bed, the women used to gather before the fireplace in the living room, and there Eleanor would read aloud for an hour or two. That August she read Henry Adams. She and FDR had known him in Washington, had lunched and dined in his Lafayette Square house, and she told a little of what he was personally like before reading portions of his *Education* and *Mont-Saint-Michel and Chartres*. She also read David Grayson (Ray Stannard Baker), whose *The Country-man's Year* contained a sentence she read with special emphasis and repeated several times: "Back of tranquillity lies always conquered unhappiness."

F O U R

I**F THERE** is doubt about the date of the decision to build the cottage at Val Kill, there is none whatever about the dates of the actual planning and construction.

From late winter and through the spring of 1925, the planning of this vital enterprise was the dominant private interest of the three friends—and in it, FDR, who loved to design and build things, was increasingly involved. In February and March he made his second extended cruise aboard the *Larooco* in Florida waters. But he arranged by letter for a meeting of Nancy and Marion with his contractor friend Brown, and in reply to Nancy's report of this meeting, addressed himself to "Dear Nan; also Marion" from Long Key, Florida. "I knew you would adore Elliott Brown," he wrote. "He is one of the nicest people in the world, and I certainly vote for including him in our gang. It seems to me that . . . [his] suggestions are all to the good, and I am particularly pleased that Elliott's figure of $8,000 is so low. . . ." And he went on into a detailed discussion of the suggested contractual arrangements. He concluded: "We await Eleanor on Sunday [she was en route to Florida for her first experience of *Larooco* life] and I only wish that she could stay more than 10 days. She will certainly get lots of sleep and reading down here. There is no possibility of keeping her from getting tired in New York. The only way is to plan to get her away from New York and when the cottage is built that will be one means toward the end. A great deal of love to both. I wish you could be here too. Perhaps next year we can make it a real family party."

But he was not satisfied with the plans embodied in the model Nan had made. Neither was Henry Toombs, a cousin of Caroline O'Day's, who was a draftsman at the world-famous architectural firm of Mc-Kim, Mead and White, as was Marion's good friend Eric Gugler, and who spent a weekend at Hyde Park in the late spring or early summer. Toombs established an immediate rapport with FDR. A most personable young man, he was of the historically famous Toombs family of Georgia, and FDR already felt a commitment to Georgia because of Warm Springs, where he had spent nearly all of April. Its naturally heated mineral waters were doing his legs more good, he was convinced, than anything else he had tried, and he was already planning to buy its rundown resort and transform it into a polio treatment center. Toombs offered his services as Val Kill architect to Nancy, Marion, and Eleanor. The three happily accepted, and thereafter Toombs and FDR worked together as an architectural team on the project.

By then, at another picnic—this one in June of 1925—the idea for Val-Kill Industries had been born. Gathered at Val Kill that day were Nancy, Marion, Eleanor, and Caroline O'Day, who later became an honorary vice-president of the enterprise, along with two or three of the Roosevelt sons, each with a friend or two. While the children played, the four women were stimulated by the lovely rural setting, and by their plans for the cottage here, to talk of the economically determined tendency of country people, especially the young, to forsake their native farms and villages and flock into great cities, whose constantly accelerating growth constituted a grave threat to the well-being of the Republic. Franklin Roosevelt had said in public speech that the national health required a "nice balance" between industry and agriculture, and that "the growth of cities while the country population stands still," as revealed in the 1920 census, "will eventually bring disaster to the United States." Eleanor said to her three friends that day that she and her husband had "often wondered if it would be possible to establish some small industries in local areas" that would provide income for local men who could not make a living, or all their living, out of agriculture, and that would also "provide interests for bored rural women." Perhaps by such means the present disastrous trend could be halted, even reversed.

It was at that point that Nancy Cook, who "had a longing to go back to her wood-working which she had taught before the war" (as Eleanor later wrote), made her memorable suggestion: "Why not start a small factory and copy early American furniture, doing it as nearly as possible in the same way as the early Americans did it? Why not do it right here, when our cottage is built?" A cottage industry! A possible pilot project for other communities across the land! With mounting excitement that day, Nancy's idea was explored. Eleanor said she was sure that "Franklin will approve"—and he did, most heartily, when the idea was discussed with him a little later.

As for the cottage itself, they all quickly agreed that it should be built of fieldstone and should be of traditional Hudson River Dutch farmhouse design. Toombs departed from this design to the extent of including a tall, south-facing window in the living room, with a curved instead of a flat top. FDR made strong objection to this. He also objected to having the ridgepole of the ell at the same height as the ridgepole of the main house. It ought to be "without fail" one foot lower, he insisted. "If you build it that way," he threatened the three women, "I'll *never* come to visit you!" The design was of course changed as he wished.

When the final plans were submitted to contractors for construction bids, the lowest of these seemed exorbitant to FDR and Toombs,

45

although Nancy and Marion, eager for their own home, indicated an inclination to pay the extra cost. Finally FDR said, "If you three girls will just go away and leave us alone, Henry and I will build the cottage." He was sure, he said, that Henry and he could save them a great deal of money.

So "the girls" drove the long trip up to Campobello, taking along the boys and camping on the way—and within a day or so after their arrival they received a report from FDR in a letter to "Dearest Babs" ("Babs" was his nickname for Eleanor). "Last Saturday and Sunday I shopped for lumber for the cottage—found some in Rock City (Town of Milan) some in Rhinebeck—some in Poughkeepsie—average cost 50% less than Babcock [who had been low bidder for the total construction job] figures. . . ."

More detailed was his letter of the following week. Some excerpts:

"Van Aken is considered first class for stone work. Eylers is considered ditto for carpentry. P. C. Doherty is the plumber who works for Vassar College and, as his father and grandfather were the gardeners for my uncle, and great-grandfather, he will take a personal interest.

"I have written to Mr. Gay at Rock City . . . to mail you a small piece of the tulip poplar proposed for interior trim. It is a beautiful close-grained satiny wood and takes a stain wonderfully without any filler. I saw Frank Masters' den at Copake Falls done in it and it is lovely. Also, it does not split or chip like birch.

"As you will see from the above time schedule I will be here [in Hyde Park] until the stone work is approved and starts to rise [he was to go in late August to Louis Howe's little summer cottage at Horseneck Beach in Massachusetts, at the lower end of Buzzards Bay] and I will be back before it is finished. In the meantime Henry will come up once or twice to see that the preparation of the timbers and other lumber is proceeding according to Hoyle. I have got some very fine bids by shopping around for this lumber.

"On this bid of ours you will save $4,326 over Babcock's bid. His bid of $15,500 did not include the doors and trim which were $826

46

extra. On the inclosed [*sic*] bill I have not included old Pete's work around the place this winter and spring. This totals about $240, but as it is for the general improvement of my farm I think I should bear this cost. This autumn we will mark out your property and from that time on you 3 can jolly well foot the bills!

"The swimming pool is completed except for a little work to tighten the bottom [water diverted from Val Kill was used in this pool]. The ground around it is all graded, the new road south of the pool is laid out, graded and gravelled. Grass seed will go on in a few days.

"In closing, I can only suggest that hereafter you call Father the 'Cascaret'—he works while you sleep."

There came also to the island, and remains in Marion's possession, a mysterious letter from FDR about Louis Howe—dated Tuesday, July 21, 1925, addressed to "Dearest E," and marked ("Private—in part!"): "Your two good letters I found on arrival last night. Louis had gone to bed so I didn't hear about the 'operation' till this morning. It appears that Dr. Lewis, the operator was to go to Europe this week and it had to be done Sat. or not at all—he [Louis] spent Friday at the Beach, making last will, writing letters, etc., telephoned Mary [Louis' daughter] at Newport he was going to Boston to have a 'minor operation,' & told Ed. Hartley [Louis' brother-in-law?] the truth & found out from him that Grace [Louis' wife] would be well provided for if he did not survive. Then he went up to the Mass. Homeopathic Hospital, spent the night & Sat. A.M. went on the operating table with 3 anaesthetists in attendance—They gave him gas, he went under quietly, then they gave him the ether & his heart stopped. He was to all intents and purposes 'dead.' They worked over him for two hours, using every known restorative, & as there was no sign of life they gave him up & started to send a telegram announcing his death. Then he came to of his own accord, blinked an eye & in apparently a few seconds was perfectly all right again. He was of course sick & considerable shaken, spent that day & Sunday in the Hospital and came on to N.Y. with a trained nurse on the Sunday night train. So there was no operation! He has persuaded the doctors to let him work it out as he did the previous attack [?], but to give him something to make him sleep when the pain is very bad. He seems perfectly all right today but is taking it easy. . . ." FDR went on to speak of the progress being made on construction of the cottage, closing: "Loads of love to you all—it will take you a whole evening to read this. By the way, Louis wants no one told about his narrow escape!"

On Campobello the summer island life went on for the three friends and two boys in much the same way as it had done the previous year and the year before. The return trip in the first days of September, however, was rendered strenuous by the incessant quarrelsome activity of the two boys, as the trip up had been. ("I knew you three older ones would find it awfully strenuous!" FDR had written. "Those kids are made of steel and rubber.") At Boston, as Marion remembers it, the two boys were sent on to Hyde Park by train. She, Nancy, and Eleanor drove on down to Horseneck Beach, where FDR then was with Louis Howe in his summer cottage.

This cottage was a plain, square, two-story structure set against a grass-tufted sand dune and with its front porch only a few dozen yards up a gently sloping beach from high-tide waters. The three women pitched their tent on the dune (the house was much too small to accommodate them along with Louis, FDR, and the "very nice colored man" who had been hired to care for FDR). It was a starkly simple, utterly isolated life. There was no telephone in the cottage, and no other human habitation was in sight: FDR could crawl from porch to water's edge with none to see save those at the cottage, and he did so every day with great heaves of his powerful arms and shoulders, dragging behind him across the sand his withered legs. "I love it!" he called out gaily.

When the three women left after two or three days, they yet believed that FDR would be back in Hyde Park to oversee the completion of the cottage. But a few days later he arranged to become one of four polio-crippled patients of a neurologist named William McDonald, who was reported to have achieved astonishing cures of paralysis by means of

48

special exercises he had devised. McDonald lived in Marion, some dozen miles up Buzzards Bay, and FDR was to move into a small house in that village and remain there, under the doctor's supervision, for several weeks.

"You doubtless have heard of the new Doc who is to give me a strenuous course of exercises," he wrote from Horseneck Beach to "Dearest Nan (& Marion if she[s] still with you)." He was eager for the arrival of Eleanor for a visit because then he would "hear all about the house. . . . & I feel very badly that I won't see it now till the end of September. . . . Still there should be nothing to delay things—the only necessity is for Clinton to get lumber to the carpenter in time for the latter to mill it & the plumber up when things are ready for him. In regard to the shop [it was at that time intended to have the furniture workshop in the cottage] I suggest as little as possible be done till you actually live in the house & see for yourself where you fit things in. . . . It has been lovely here—Louis and I keeping real bachelor hall! Water too rough to swim these last two days but I crawl around the sand." Louis had excellent wood-working tools at Horseneck Beach; FDR made use of them. "I have made a mahogany book case (hanging) & am finishing a wonderful tool chest which I need at Hyde Park," he concluded in a prideful report to a fellow craftsman.

Two weeks later he wrote Nancy from Marion, Massachusetts, that he was "*so* glad the walls are nearly up & wild that I can't be there every weekend to watch the [house-building] progress." The progress he was making in his own leg-rebuilding was too great, however, for him even to consider a break in the McDonald routine. "Old legs are coming on finely," he said—"I can *almost* stand up without braces— another two weeks will win that trick I think—& then comes the effort to learn to walk." But he continued to keep close track of the cottage construction. He arranged to have as much of the lumber as possible —ridgepoles, rafters, flooring—come from trees grown on his own land, charging somewhat less for these logs than would have to be paid elsewhere. Part of the payment for him was the great pleasure he derived from his sense of the cottage's organic connection with the Hyde Park soil—of its fieldstone and wood being literally an outgrowth of earth he owned and loved.

His exercise treatments at Marion were maintained uninterrupted for more than three months, at the end of which he was able to walk— to make his way upright, at any rate—for nearly one hundred yards with a brace on his left leg only, a cane propping his right. He returned to Hyde Park overjoyed in early December. He proclaimed that within a year or so he would throw away both braces forever and walk with, at worst, a slight limp—though as it turned out, says Marion sadly, he had by then reached the limit of his improvement.

By Christmas Day, 1925, the cottage—Val Kill Cottage, they now dubbed it—was virtually completed. And in bright sunshine on New Year's Day, 1926, the cottage was "officially" opened with a dinner party to which the entire Roosevelt family came, including Granny and nineteen-year-old Anna. They ate off a table improvised of raw lumber resting on sawhorses, they sat on small kegs—but this seemed only to add to the informal gaiety. FDR had found somewhere a small children's book published early in the century entitled *Little Marion's Pilgrimage*, and this he presented to Marion with a flourish, having inscribed on its flyleaf: "For my little Pilgrim, whose Progress is always Upward and Onward, to the Things of Beauty and the Thoughts of Love, and of Light, from her affectionate Uncle Franklin. On the occasion of the opening of the Love Nest on the Val Kill. January 1, 1926."

A little over four weeks later, Eleanor went by train with him to Florida for the third, and as it turned out, the last cruise of the *Larooco*.* She didn't want to go. En route she wrote to "Dearest Marion" to thank her for her parting gifts of a "pillow which I've enjoyed all day & the chocolate which F & I have both been eating! . . . I assure

---

* The boat was driven far inland, and deposited there, on the flood that accompanied the terrific hurricane of September 1926. It was sold as junk in 1927.

50

you when I left I felt anything but merry—I would be having such a good time if you two & my two little boys were along & as it is I've just tried hard to forget how much I am missing you." She had finished reading Christopher Morley's new novel, *Thunder on the Left*. She had found it "strange and imaginative," she wrote, "giving me a horrid feeling of impotence & unrest as tho' the web of life must beat us all & yet I read every word which as you know is strange for me!" William Hart, owner of a cottage in which FDR had lived at Warm Springs, boarded the train at Savannah "& F & he have talked 'Warm Springs' every minute & will till we reach Jacksonville at 10 P.M.!" (Eleanor had grave doubts about this Warm Springs venture, in which FDR planned to invest two-thirds of his total fortune; if it failed, as so many of his business speculations had, he might be financially unable to finance his children's college education.) The country she had looked out upon that morning "was desolate. . . ." And she closed: "Dear Marion, I love you & miss you sadly, someday we must all go on a real pleasure trip. I'm so tired of doing just what I'm doing now! Much much love."

Six days later she wrote Marion from aboard the *Larooco:*

"We are having a killing time with our engines & are now on our way to Miami but tied up to the mango bushes in one of the passages while they find out why our clutch is slipping. My face is covered with mosquito bites in spite of citronella & my only fear is that when we reach Miami they'll think I have small pox!

"Florida is queerer each year & the people make me long to know why they are here. We have a mechanic on the boat today who brought his wife because they're living in a tent & I suspect she wouldn't be left alone. Well, she's a little German dressmaker and the most unhappy, out of place person, now what is she doing here?

"We're off again! I wish you were here, it would do you good & you should enjoy it. The canal comes out here right on the ocean & even I have to acknowledge it is pretty! There is just the strip of sand & palm trees & a few bushes between us & the ocean & on the other side they've cut the mangroves & are drying the land & I suppose people will build houses there! [The Florida land boom of the twenties was then at its fantastic height.]

"Franklin is trying to walk on deck & it seems to go quite well so I hope he'll do it every day. . . .

"Much love to Nan and to you, life is quite empty without your dear presence."

Meanwhile, in New York, Marion was making a major career decision. Miss Todhunter was planning to retire and return to her native England at the end of the 1927 school year; she wished Marion, now associate principal of the school, to become its new owner and principal, and Marion had never wanted anything more. But she couldn't raise enough money to buy the school alone. Neither could she and Nancy do so together. Whereupon Eleanor, who had of course been involved in these discussions, became intensely interested. The great heroine and educative experience of her adolescence had been Mlle. Marie Souvestre, a remarkable Frenchwoman in whose Allenswood School, in England, she was enrolled for three years. She felt that if she could ever do for others even a portion of what Mlle. Souvestre had done for her, she would be a success in life. And so she spiritually jumped at the chance of becoming an active partner in the Todhunter enterprise, putting up a third of the purchase money and, as Marion was eager to have her do, teaching in the school or even becoming associate principal. But there must be a time lag, Eleanor pointed out, for she could not fully embark on this new project, nor make a more than "possible" commitment of money, until her youngest son, John, entered Groton in the fall of 1928. Hence her response to a letter in which Marion told of being offered by Miss Todhunter the opportunity to take over as principal in the fall of 1927, with a promise to buy the school later if that became financially possible for her.

"Marion dearest," wrote Eleanor from Miami on February 9, ". . . I think you ought to take the 1st place for the first year with the understanding that you have no financial responsibility. It will be easier for you to settle in that way & when Miss Todhunter . . . de-

52

part[s] then I'll slip in & do all I can for you but I feel strongly that you have to find out gradually what I can do. The one or two afternoons a week [of teaching] sound easy . . . but associate principals for the good of the School should have college degrees & I think I'd better be something less high sounding!" She wanted no pay "the first year," she wrote, "as I would consider that I was being paid in experience & the next year if we assumed joint financial responsibility then we could arrange some percent of profit after your salary & all expenses were paid. I think it will be quite thrilling . . . & I know you can make a great success. It is going to be such fun to work with you & Nan & you are dears to let me join in it all for I'd never have had the initiative or the ability in any one line to have done anything interesting alone!"

The "various vicissitudes incident to life on the bounding deep" continued not to her liking. Two guests had joined the cruise, and "Franklin has just heard the Moseleys are coming [these were Sir Oswald Moseley, who later became head of the British Union of Fascists, and Lady Cynthia Moseley] so we are going to be quite crowded on board & I may try to leave Thursday night, the day Missy arrives as I don't know where she will sleep if I don't! I'm sleeping on deck." She closed, "Much much love dear."

Eleanor did entrain for New York on the day after Missy LeHand came aboard the *Larooco* at Key Largo. She was eager to get away— eager to rejoin her two dearest friends and enter again into the active, interesting, useful life she shared with them.

F I V E

V A L K I L L Cottage was the center of the living world for Marion and Nancy. The two kept their Greenwich Village apartment, but it was merely a place to stay until, their work-week city commitments fulfilled, they could "go home" to Val Kill. The cottage was also a vital center of Eleanor's world. It became the place she lived in whenever she could and for as long a time as she could. She was happy there as nowhere else.

She had never liked nor felt at home in the house on East Sixty-fifth Street. It had been a "Christmas present to Franklin and Eleanor from Mama" in 1907. Eleanor had been neither consulted nor fully informed concerning its design and construction in 1908. She had always resented this, along with the fact that Sara Delano Roosevelt retained legal title to the purported "gift" and to the house next door, built at the same time, which was her own city home. As for the Hyde Park mansion, Eleanor had always felt herself to be, at best, a permanent guest there, and at times an unwelcome one. She was reluctant to invite people there without first obtaining her mother-in-law's permission, and she knew that the aristocratic Sara strongly disapproved of the manners and opinions of some of the friends she had made through her political and civic organizational activities. Only at Campobello had she felt that she lived in a house of her own, for her husband had clear legal title to this property. But Campobello was only a summer place, after all, and—here again—she had had nothing whatever to do with designing it or even with the decision to purchase it. Sara had decided to buy it, and presented it to Franklin as—uniquely—an outright gift, no strings attached.

Hence Eleanor's joy in Val Kill Cottage.

The sharing of it with her dearest friends did nothing to reduce—on the contrary, it greatly enhanced—her feeling that here, at last, she had a home of her own. Her emotional dependence upon these friends, closely joined to a rebellious feminism, was at its greatest at this time, and remained so for some years. Typical was a letter she wrote Marion in 1925. "I wish you & Nan were here," she wrote. "I feel I'd like to go off with you and forget the rest of the world existed. . . . Marion dearest I love & miss you & no amount of excitement could make me miss you less." Typical also was her comment upon a luncheon conversation she and Rose Schneiderman, who was visiting her, had had with her two youngest sons. It was, she wrote Marion, "a discussion on trade unions & R was left as I always am with the boys, feeling quite impotent to make a dent, because they regard me as a woman to be dutifully and affectionately thought of because I am their mother but even tho' I hold queer opinions they can't be considered seriously as against those of their usual male environment!"

She at once made it clear to Granny that the cottage was a separate, private establishment—that there were now two independent households at Hyde Park. Granny perforce accepted the new arrangement, and with outward grace, whatever her inner feelings. On April 2, 1926, Granny wrote her son, who had just gone to Warm Springs for a month, saying that Anna was staying in the Big House (so it was now designated, to distinguish it from the cottage), as was Anna's fiancé, a thirty-year-old stockbroker named Curtis Dall. Eleanor with Brother and John were staying at the cottage, "but they came over here for some hours today and tomorrow they will have lunch here. We three are invited for supper tomorrow at the cottage and they all lunch here on Sunday. Eleanor is so happy over there that she looks well and plump, don't tell her so, it is very becoming. . . ."

That spring and summer the cottage grounds were landscaped—with Nancy planning and supervising it all and doing not a little of the physical labor. A flower garden and a kitchen garden were planted, and a beautifully grassed and tree-shaded picnic area was developed, having at its north end a large stone fireplace where hamburgers, hot dogs, steaks, and other food could be cooked. Later, because FDR was forever complaining that no one cooked things the way he wanted them cooked (few shared his taste for meat almost raw), Nancy made a small grill, which was placed beside his permanently assigned picnic chair. On it he could, and happily did thereafter, cook things "properly."

Simultaneous with the initial yard work in 1926 was the making of the first Val-Kill furniture. The seemingly indefatigable Nan and a single workman, in a workroom that had been designed into the cottage as the manufacturing plant of the proposed Val-Kill Industries, turned out through the middle months of 1926 all the beds, tables, chairs, chests, and so on needed to furnish the cottage. The workroom was adequate for this, but not for the larger purpose of manufacturing furniture for sale, as was at once realized. Then it was that Eleanor financed the construction of a separate workshop back of the cottage, with all three women joining equally in the purchase of tools and other equipment.

A number of highly skilled local cabinetmakers of Italian and Norwegian descent were eventually hired, but "Nan was the master craftsman, under whom the others worked," as Marion says, recalling the shop as a light and airy place, filled with the soft, pungent odor of

56

freshly sawed wood. She and Eleanor spent hours at a time there, watching with fascination the loving skill with which the turnings were made and the staining and polishing done. Some of Nan's designs came from Monticello, to which the three friends made pilgrimage "as ardent disciples of Thomas Jefferson" and where Nan made careful drawings of three pieces in particular—the chair in which Jefferson sat as he did his architectural drawings for the University of Virginia, the table with a movable top on which he spread his drawings so that he could bring them to him without rising from the chair (Nan reproduced the table and chair for FDR), and a music rack "for people to use for their magazines."

Because of the cottage, by means of the cottage, the lives of the three friends became more closely intertwined than ever.

It was in the cottage one night in 1926 ("—we were sitting in the little room which had the seats beside the fireplace," Marion recalls) that Eleanor told her two friends of the deepest, most secret of all the hurts she had suffered in her life, the hurt at which she had hinted several times before.

She told of her husband's emotional involvement with a young woman, Lucy Mercer, whom she had employed as her social secretary when Franklin was Assistant Secretary of the Navy—told how, after a long period of agonized doubt and suspicion, she had discovered irrefutable proof of the involvement, through letters found in her husband's luggage when he returned from a mission to war-torn Europe desperately ill with double pneumonia in the fall of 1918. She told, too, of her offer to him of a divorce and of how this was refused, in family conclave, for several reasons: Lucy was a Catholic and the Church forbade marriage with a divorced man; Granny threatened to disinherit her son; Franklin protested his abiding love for her, Eleanor, and the children; a divorce would be fatal to his political career. Franklin and Lucy had pledged their word of honor not to see one another again, and two years later Lucy had married Winthrop Rutherfurd, a wealthy widower old enough to be her father, a man of distinguished family whom Eleanor and Franklin had long known as a casual social acquaintance.

Eleanor spoke of these things quite calmly and even matter-of-factly—almost as if she described a natural phenomenon, something that happened because the world and the people in it are as they are and move as they do. As they must. Yet Marion and Nancy both knew that this was not really the way she felt, deep down. They sensed her feeling that she had been personally betrayed and profoundly insulted ("—she had been raised with the highest Victorian ideals of fidelity," says Marion) and worse, that the betrayal and insult were at least partially the result of her own inadequacy as a wife and as a woman. They sensed that she had deliberately chosen a calmly neutral response because a different one, dictated by her deepest feeling, would have destroyed her utterly and gravely wounded innocent people. Her response was, in other words, an act of will ("back of tranquillity lies always conquered unhappiness"); and part and parcel of it was a determination *not* to force her friends into taking sides with her against her husband, but instead to accept the situation as it was and him as he wanted and even needed to be. Clear, if wholly tacit, was the understanding that one overriding reason for doing this derived from FDR's high destiny. To a varying degree, but surely, they all had *historical* responsibilities.

And so this intimate disclosure, which was not spoken of again—and of which no whisper escaped the cottage—had no deleterious effect upon Marion's and Nancy's relationship with FDR. It may even have enriched that relationship by deepening its basis for sympathetic understanding. Certainly it caused no loss of personal respect for FDR. He never betrayed any awareness that they might have been told about his love affair, though he could not but have guessed it, in view of his wife's intimacy with them. To no one, indeed, did he ever communicate *himself* in the way Eleanor communicated *herself* to her two intimates that night. In this respect, his difference from his wife was profound. As her life went on, she deliberately, if also compulsively, revealed much of herself as honestly as she could to a large public; she permitted herself to be almost fully known to several for whom she cared deeply. He, on the other hand, made intimate revelations rarely, to a very few, and then inadvertently. (Aside from Eleanor and Louis, Missy was perhaps unique in witnessing him in his occasional moods of total black depression; on the *Larooco* sometimes, after a bad psychological night, he remained in his cabin until noon, unable till then to face with a proper hearty cheeriness the guests he almost always had aboard.) He permitted himself to be fully known to no one at all.

Several months later there arose a misunderstanding between FDR and Marion-and-Nancy over who was responsible for certain expenses and upkeep at Val Kill. Marion wrote FDR a letter stiff with hurt, suggesting termination of the entire arrangement, since he was evidently displeased with it, and with them. His prompt reply put everything right—and better than before.

He wrote: "Do you know that I am dumbfounded by your letter? And frankly surprised and upset that you should swallow what that doddering old idiot Clinton tells you without coming to me & asking the truth. . . . I never told Clinton I would not pay for cleaning out the pool. He never spoke of it. He asked me for a 'little money ahead,'—i.e. a loan against future work & I refused. He asked if I would pay for the bridge repairs and I said that he would have to take it up with Miss Cook, as Eleanor had told me that I should pay nothing for that as it was up to Clinton to make it right.

"You are right. I assume the upkeep and repair of the pool and have always done so.

"So what is it all about? Why the injured tone . . . Oh ye of little faith! Don't you poor idiots realize how much I care for you both and love having you at Val Kill! . . .

"Think it over, my dears, stop talking about 'cheapening our relations,' stop listening to fairy stories, . . . get your feet on earth and be your own dear straight forward nice selves. . . . If I had you here I would spank you both and then kiss you."

It was now clear to Marion and Nancy why Eleanor and Franklin lived separate lives, having only such relations as law or business partners might have in an enterprise absorbingly interesting to them both—partners who were also good social friends. For they *were* friends as well as teammates in politics. They had enormous mutual respect—Eleanor for Franklin's optimistic courage, creative energy, patience, political sagacity; Franklin for Eleanor's high-mindedness, compassionate humanitarianism, sound judgment, absolute integrity— and they generally enjoyed one another in social situations.

It was clear, too, why Eleanor displayed nothing of what Marion calls the "belittling emotion of jealousy" concerning her husband's constant work-and-play companionship with Missy LeHand. She believed Lucy to be the one great romantic love of her husband's life. She was sure that no one, certainly not Missy, could take Lucy's place with him. And she of course recognized that his physical condition and the effort he made to improve it while simultaneously advancing his political career and fulfilling his business obligations (he was vice-president in charge of the New York office of the Fidelity and Deposit Company of Maryland; he was a partner with Basil O'Connor in the law firm of Roosevelt and O'Connor) necessitated his having a secretary who was always at hand and could do for him many things a secretary would not ordinarily do. This in turn required a special psychological relationship, one of total personal commitment on the secretary's part.

Sometimes, in later years, Eleanor would be resentful of Missy's assumption of hostessing duties and functions she thought she herself ought to perform, though Missy never did so unless it was FDR's desire. More often Eleanor was mildly irritated by Missy's wholly uncritical (as she felt) devotion to FDR. The younger woman's invariably smiling submissiveness to his thought and will, even to his wish and whim, was excessive, in Eleanor's view, and sometimes encouraged him in directions she deemed unfortunate. This was so with regard to Warm Springs. But such irritations and resentments were surface ripples upon the broad stream of Eleanor's personal affection for the younger woman—a stream that flowed for as long as they both lived and that had in it mingled currents of gratitude and pity. She pitied Missy for submitting so eagerly, so unwittingly—as Eleanor thought—to what seemed to her a quite ruthless exploitation. She was grateful to Missy for a service to FDR that relieved her, Eleanor, of burdens, obligations restrictive upon her own independent life. She had been more than willing to be relieved by Missy of the necessity to cruise for weeks on end aboard the *Larooco* along a coast she found "eerie and menacing." She was more than willing to be relieved of the necessity to keep house in Warm Springs.

FDR went to Warm Springs with Missy, following his third *Larooco* cruise. He spent April of 1926 there, exercising daily for hours in the pool and making final arrangements for his investment there (he signed the legal purchase agreement on April 29). Eleanor came down for a visit. No more than before was she taken with the place. She actively disliked the slovenliness and poverty of rural Georgia; she could hardly bear with adequate politeness the racism of some of her Georgia hosts and hostesses; and she continued openly to disapprove of her husband's purchase decision. ("Missy . . . is keen about everything here of course!" she wrote, rather acidly, to Marion.) She continued so to disapprove—that is, until the afternoon of April 24.

On that afternoon she "had a long talk with Franklin," as she wrote to Marion next day, and found that her negative attitude toward his Warm Springs enterprise, joined to his mother's and to a degree, his law partner's, had hurt him deeply and was dangerously lowering his morale. ". . . he feels . . . that he's trying to do a big thing which may be a financial success & a medical and philanthropic opportunity for infantile & that all of us have raised our eyebrows & thrown cold water on it. There is nothing to do but to make him feel one is interested & to try to keep his points before him 1st that he must use it in winter himself 2nd that he cannot honorably neglect the F & D because of Mr. Black's kindness to him [Van Lear Black was president of Fidelity and Deposit and had refused to accept FDR's resignation following the polio attack; indeed, had insisted upon continuing his full salary of $25,000 per annum]. . . . Henry [Toombs, who was to serve as Warm Springs architect] arrives tonight—Franklin is expecting to leave here May 5th. . . . He will return here for a week in August either with Elliott or me & won't that be a hot little jaunt!"

On the day following this letter she wrote again to "Dearest Marion": "You can't think how good it was to hear from you & Nan this morning. I'm glad you missed me for I thought of all you must be doing & wished I could be there. Henry . . . & F. are discussing plans. . . . Tomorrow p.m. [April 27, 1926] we drive to Atlanta for F. to talk to the Dr.'s convention about this place. [At the American Orthopedic Association's annual convention in Atlanta FDR initiated the process that culminated in official medical approval of Warm Springs as a polio treatment and research center]." She could hardly wait to get away. "I'm looking forward to seeing you next Sunday at supper," she closed. (On May 4, a few days after her return from Warm Springs, she wrote her husband: ". . . I know how you love creative work, my only feeling is that Georgia is somewhat distant for you to keep in touch with what is really a big undertaking. One cannot, it seems to me, have *vital* interests in widely divided places, but that may be because I'm old and rather overwhelmed by what there is to do in one place and it wearies me to think of even undertaking to make new ties. Don't be discouraged by me; I have great confidence in your extraordinary interest and enthusiasm.")

One suspects that Eleanor would have been more than willing to have Missy relieve her of the necessity of housekeeping in Marion, Massachusetts, where FDR had his second course of treatments under Dr. McDonald in the summer of 1926. She went to that village in mid-May to look at the house they would rent there, and wrote next day from Dedham to "Marion dearest": "The house in Marion is cunning but I think will be hot & it is going to take some managing to get everyone in. The water supply is uncertain as to quantity I gather & it is quite a ways into Marion & will require much going back & forth, but of course it can be made possible as it is really very comfortable for Franklin but I can't say I look forward to it as restfull [*sic*]!" (This letter began: ". . . I hate to think you've been unhappy dear, it is new for me to have anyone know when I have 'moods' much less have it

62

make any real difference & if you'll try not to take them too seriously I'll try not to let myself have them! I wish you were coming with Nan to-morrow, it doesn't seem quite right to be seeing things without you—I'll go straight to the office [of the State Democratic Committee] from the train on Thursday & hope to have a glimpse of you dear—")

Her anticipation of no "restfull" time in Marion was abundantly justified in the event. Indeed, the whole of that summer of 1926 **was** an unusually crowded one. In early June was the wedding, in Hyde Park, of Anna and Curtis Dall. ("Missy is delighted to be going to you for the wedding," Eleanor had written Marion from Warm Springs in April; Missy stayed with Nan and Marion in Val Kill Cottage for this occasion.) In the following weeks was completed the formal legal establishment of the Georgia Warm Springs Foundation (FDR was president, Basil O'Connor secretary-treasurer, Louis Howe a director). Then to Marion, Massachusetts, where the tremendous physical strenuousness of Dr. McDonald's treatments (FDR exercised hours daily within a "walking board" the doctor had devised) was accompanied by an equally strenuous political activity. For FDR, at Al Smith's request, was to be temporary chairman and deliver the keynote address at the New York State Democratic Convention in late September, and was under strong pressure, which he successfully resisted, to accept nomination for the U.S. Senate in that convention. This added dozens of letters daily to his load of Warm Springs correspondence and required of Eleanor the entertainment of an incessant stream of politicians.

Yet Marion Dickerman, who with Nancy came to the Marion house for several long weekends, remembers that summer as a "very happy" one on the whole "because we all felt that we were moving toward a great future."

Warm Springs was FDR's dominant interest during the months that followed. He entrained for Warm Springs a few days after the state Democratic convention ended, taking with him not only Missy but his mother—Granny stayed for two weeks, during which she developed no fondness for the place or the project—and remained there until after election day, while Eleanor, with Nancy and Marion—to the extent that her Todhunter duties permitted—worked in the state Democratic campaign (Robert F. Wagner gave Eleanor much credit for his victory in the race for U.S. Senator). And Warm Springs was also a dominant interest of the aborning Val-Kill Industries during these same months. Nancy and her workers in the shop, though concerned to manufacture enough pieces for the first Val-Kill sales showing in the spring of 1927, gave first priority to the making of the furniture for FDR's newly built Warm Springs cottage.

He was delighted with the fruits of Nancy's labors when he returned to Warm Springs in February. He wrote his mother that "the new furniture fits perfectly and is just the right color," while Eleanor, who went down with him and Missy, reported to "Nan dearest" that she had "put all the beds up yesterday, & today the table & box came & they are both in the room & you can't think how lovely they all look—Franklin is delighted with them and can hardly wait to get in." She transmitted to Nancy his wish for another chest of drawers and a folding table. "Now will you figure on a low chest for the little guest-room, like this [she submitted a crude drawing]. . . . Also a chest of drawers for Missy's room . . . [and] for Missy's room a little bed table with shelf." She added that they had "all bathed this morning & the air is very soft. . . ." She continued, however, actively to dislike the place.

"I think what I hate down here is the untidiness & the pressure all about one, the hotel, cottages, woods, porch, everything untidy & everyone apparently oblivious to the cans & dirt!" she wrote. "However, it is better than it used to be & when the roads dry & harden the new [cottages] . . . F. has built & the golf course will be very pretty."

Again she was eager to return to New York ("I miss you so much. . . . I shall be keen to hear about everything").

For she was truly happy during these years only when she was with her two closest friends—and happiest when with them at Val Kill Cottage. It was to them, and to the cottage, that she came when troubled in her relations with Granny, as she very often was, and in her relations with her husband, as she was—overtly, acutely—far less frequently. "We always tried to help her in every way we could, and also to build a bridge back to him," Marion says, in reference to the fact that she and Nancy were, at Eleanor's own tacit insistence, *his* friends as well as hers and could therefore themselves serve as a bridge.

Ordinarily, when he was at the Big House at Hyde Park, Eleanor stayed there, too—but one summer evening she left him there and came, distraught, to the cottage. The "misunderstanding" that time was serious. She "remained closeted with us for three days," as Marion vividly remembers. Finally, Nan telephoned FDR at the Big House and spoke with some sternness.

"If you are wise you will come over here," she said, "and right away!"

"But will she talk to me?" he asked.

"You come!"

He did, in the Ford with hand controls he had had specially built for his use, and he parked in the drive before the cottage. But once there he could only sit and wait helplessly, it being utterly impossible for him to move himself unaided from a sitting to an upright position, his feet on the ground, his leg braces locked in place; and perhaps it was Eleanor's increasingly poignant sense of his utter helplessness at this juncture that pierced at last the wall of hurt hostility she had raised against him. She went out to the car. She sat with him there for a long time—more than two hours, Marion believes—but then she went back with him to the Big House, and the quarrel was not mentioned again.

The Cuff Links Club celebrates FDR's birthday at the White House, 1934. The theme, arranged by Louis Howe, was a parody of opponents' charges that President Roosevelt was behaving like a Roman emperor. Seated, l. to r.: Missy LeHand, Malvina Thompson, FDR, Margaret Durand, Stanley Prenosil. Standing: Marvin McIntyre, Grace Tully, Thomas Lynch, Kirk Simpson, Nancy Cook, Eleanor Roosevelt, Anna Roosevelt, Irvin McDuffie (FDR's valet), Charles McCarthy, James Sullivan, Marion Dickerman, Louis Howe, Steve Early.

Buzzards Bay, Summer, 1925

Louis Howe's camp at Horseneck Beach
where he helped IDR begin his recovery from polio: Louis Howe, his
daughter Mary, and IDR, Jr.

(ABOVE) Eleanor and Marion by the
garden fence, at IDR's rented
cottage in Marion, Mass.

(LEFT) Commander Richard E.
Byrd at Marion, Mass. with
IDR, Jr. and John.

Camping trip with the boys en route to Campobello, summer, 1926.

Nancy, Marion, and Eleanor beside the touring car, packed and ready to go.

Marion tests her culinary skills on the outdoor "stove".

Picnicking on Campo: Marion, Russell (the boys' tutor), Captain Calder, FDR, Jr., Eleanor, Henry Roosevelt, John, and George Draper.

Val Kill cottage at Hyde Park

"Franklin had very strong feeling that everything had to be done in the Dutch tradition of the Hudson Valley. In Henry Toombs' sketch of Val Kill cottage, he comments in detail detail. The cottage was completed in the summer of 1925 and we celebrated with our first meal there, New Year's Day, 1926." Marion Dickerman, Memoir.

Val Kill Cottage

The frame of the cottage, abuilding.

Architect Henry Toombs and Marion reviewing the blueprints. Builder Henry Clinton and stonemason George Van Aken look on.

The living room of Val Kill cottage. The big table and the desk in the corner are Nancy Cook's designs.

Eleanor with Nancy Cook in Nan's workroom in the Val Kill shop.

Summer days at Val Kill

Planning the Women's Democratic News: Eleanor, Nancy, Caroline O'Day, and Marion. "Eleanor edited the News with Louis Howe's help I wrote the county notes. The first issue appeared in 1925, and the last in 1935."

The Cuff Links "gang" at another birthday for FDR, produced by Louis Howe at the governor's mansion, Albany, 1930.

Todhunter School

Nancy, Marion, Eleanor, Molly Goodwin, Malvina Thompson with
Todhunter girls at the White House. "As First Lady, Eleanor always
invited Todhunter School seniors to visit Washington. The girls fretted
about etiquette and once, though I signaled that it was all right to
smoke, none did. They said later 'We wanted to make you proud of us for once.'"

Eleanor conducting a class.

Eleanor with granddaughter Sistie Dall on their way to classes at Todhunter.

Todhunter girls with Eleanor and Marion in Eleanor's sitting room at the White House. "Everyone felt really welcome in the Roosevelt rooms in the White House; there was a sense of cluttered, natural comfort and democratic hospitality."

The cast of the play Louis Howe directed at Todhunter, April 1929.

Days at Campobello, 1927

The Roosevelt "Cottage" at Campobello

Captain Calder ferrying Eleanor, Nancy & Marion To the island on The <u>Scaramouche</u>.

"One day to our great amusement we looked out the window and saw three of the boys wearing tails made from seaweed to prove they were descended from monkeys – This was the time of the famous Scopes Trial in Tennessee."

Picnicking on the island. Eleanor with FDR Jr. and John, Peggy Lehenson (Marion's sister), Marion, Russell, the boys' governess Seline Thiel, James & Anna.

"Life on the water was one of the exciting parts of our plays at Campobello."

Trip abroad with the boys, 1929

FDR Jr., Marion, John and Eleanor on deck of the *Regina*.

The Buick is hoisted aboard.

Soon after sailing, Eleanor and Nancy are handed a cable from FDR, "'You left your casket,' of course meaning 'basket'. We cabled back 'No need for casket, at least not yet'."

Trip abroad with the boys, 1929

In front, the Buick; behind, a rented limousine and chauffeur. "The very stylish car resulted from a discussion between Eleanor and Granny. Eleanor declared 'I will see that your grandsons travel in a way to which you think they should be accustomed.'"

With the boys at a Belgian sidewalk café. "I had told them about the wonderful German coffee cake we would have — what was served but National Biscuit crackers!"

Eleanor and Marion sunbathing on the beach at Cherbourg.

The pool at Val Kill, 1932

Eleanor, IDR, Missy Le Hand, and Earl Miller. "Franklin took great joy in the present, and the swimming pool was a place to relax and enjoy his family and friends."

"Franklin had overcome a handicap that would have been impossible for anyone else, but he never referred to it."

Eleanor lighting Franklin's cigarette. Standing beside him, Henry Toombs, smoking his pipe, and Gus Gennerich, IDR's bodyguard.

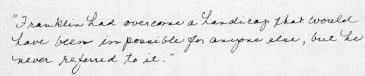

Eleanor and Anna romping on the lawn, with Caroline O'Day looking on.

Return to Campobello, June 1933

On board the Amberjack on the way to Campobello island: John,
James, FDR, Marion, FDR Jr., Eleanor, Mary Dreier, Antonia
Hatvany, Nancy with her movie camera, Frances Keller.

Franklin and Eleanor greeting Campobello friends. "Roosevelt was
buoyant. He got into the car at Welch pool and made a short
talk to his old friends and neighbors."

Return to Campobello - The picnic celebration

"Franklin always liked to have one of his boys with him for companionship and an arm to lean on. At Campobello this time it was James."

"Eleanor and Missy cooked the hot dogs. Eleanor was always happiest when she was busy."

JDR Jr.

Return to Campobello — The Picnic Celebration

Louis Howe and
Henry Morganthau Jr.

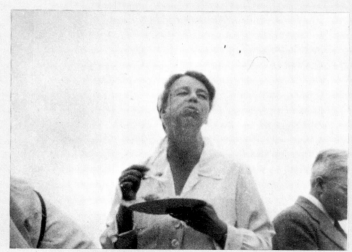

Eleanor with potato salad
on her face.

"Officers of the
Indianapolis joined
us at the beach. I'm
afraid some of the
navy men were a bit
surprised at the lack
of formality."

Visit to Arthurdale, West Virginia, 1934: the Subsistence Homestead Project

Eleanor and Marion talking with a homestead family. "One woman showed us a scrapbook she had made, 'My Dream House'. She had pasted magazine pictures of furniture and fixtures, hoping some day to own them."

One of the homestead houses. "The project failed, but the people there at least knew that their government 'cared'."

Bernard Baruch. "He contributed liberally to almost all projects that interested Eleanor."

Visit to Arthurdale, 1934

Isabella Greenway. "She helped with the project. She later voted for Wendell Willkie and even urged me to do so."

Clarence Pickett: "He was a philosopher. As head of Quakers Relief, he had interested Eleanor in the project."

Louis Howe. "Eleanor and Louis really sponsored Arthurdale in the beginning. The spirit of it, the charm of it, and some of the mistakes of it were all theirs."

Chazy Lake, 1934

"Eleanor took a small cottage at Chazy Lake in the Adirondacks. Nan and Earl Miller took along cameras and in 1934 conjured up a skit they called 'Kidnapping the First Lady.'"

Chazy Lake, 1934

Captain Blood (Earl Miller) drops his pistol and the First Lady (Eleanor) graciously retrieves it for him. Rescue arrives at last, and everyone (including the villain) dances in celebration.

Newspapermen's picnic at Val Kill, 1934

Earnest K. Lindley, reporter for the New York Herald Tribune.

Eleanor at the big fireplace.

"Oscar Chapman and Harry Hopkins did a silly little dance, wearing Franklin's bathrobes as togas."

FDR's mother, Sara Delano Roosevelt ("Granny") enjoying herself.

Newspapermen's Picnic

FDR does one of his hand tricks:
"Franklin's way of avoiding
embarrassing questions."

Henry Morgenthau Jr.
and Caroline O'Day.

Rex Tugwell

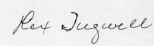

Anna at the badminton court.

Warm Springs, Georgia, 1934

Eleanor greeting crowd at railroad station. Missy is behind her.

FDR picnicking. "Warm Springs was a famous place for picnics. One had been planned the day Franklin died there."

Marion with the Roosevelt spaniel. "The Roosevelts had a series of dogs that died from over-feeding. This little spaniel did. When Fala came along, rigid diet rules were set."

Warm Springs, 1934

"Earl Miller felt horseback riding would be a good form of exercise for Franklin. He tried it several times but never was happy because he had no grip in his knees."

Eleanor by the pool.

Nancy, Missy, and Mrs. Henry Toomba

"The pool was an unending source of pleasure for the President, and woe unto you if he caught you unaware. You were in for a good dunking!"

Granny's 80th birthday party.

September, 1935

FDR and Granny, Sara
Delano Roosevelt. "Franklin
differed with his mother,
he would be annoyed with
her, but he seemed to
understand her and
have a genuine love and
affection for her, and she
for him."

In front: Ruth (Mrs.
Elliott Roosevelt), Betsy
(Mrs. James Roosevelt)
holding daughter Sara,
Sistie and Buzzy Dall
and their mother Anna.
Seated: Eleanor, Granny,
FDR. Standing: FDR Jr.,
Elliott, James and John.

The King and Queen of England visit Hyde Park, June 11, 1938

Guests will be presented to the President and
Mrs. Roosevelt and the King and Queen
immediately on arrival at the President's cottage

Guests are then requested to take seats
under the trees where luncheon will
be served to them

In the event of rain, there will be a
buffet luncheon at the big house
at one o'clock

TOP: King George VI and Queen Elizabeth with Eleanor. MIDDLE: the Queen at her table. BOTTOM: the King at his table with Granny and Gov. and Mrs. Herbert Lehman. "Though it was always called the 'hot dog picnic,' the menu included Virginia ham, turkey, sausages, strawberry cake, green salad, coffee and beer. The Queen couldn't eat hot dogs — her mouth was too small!"

Winston Churchill's visit to Val Kill, 1940

"The day Churchill visited was a scorcher, and the President looked his worst in that awful seersucker suit."

Churchill & Eleanor having a serious discussion about the war.

"Mr. Churchill jumped into the pool, just like a little kewpie - his skin as white as the driven snow."

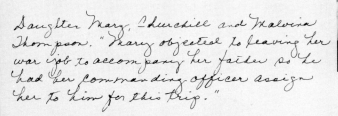

Daughter Mary, Churchill and Malvina Thompson. "Mary objected to leaving her war job to accompany her father so he had her commanding officer assign her to him for this trip."

Visiting Royalty

Princess Martha and Crown Prince Olaf of
Norway at a party in their honor, 1939.
"Princess Martha was very pretty &
gay and Franklin found her charming.
He wanted me to find her a house
nearby but I didn't succeed."

Queen Wilhelmina of the Netherlands,
visiting with daughter, Princess Juliana, and
granddaughters, Irene & Beatrice, 1941.
"Queen Wilhelmina and Franklin had a
long talk on the terrace. They agreed on
everything except colonialism."

"Everybody loved Juliana. She slipped
into the kitchen at the Val Kill Tea Shop
and whispered in Nellie Johannsen's
ear that she was expecting her third child."

"We gave the little Dutch princesses, Irene
and Beatrice clam chowder for lunch
and they showed by the faces they made
that they didn't like it.

Some other faces from the Roosevelt world...

Grover Whelan

Cordell Hull

Dorothy Backer Schiff &
Malvina Thompson

Mr. & Mrs. Harold Ickes

Josephus Daniels
Eric Zugler

Fiorello La Guardia
Frances Perkins

Fannie Hurst

Mrs. William Randolph Hearst

Mrs. "Rosy" Roosevelt

Raymond Moley

Steve Early

George Backer & Sam Rosenman

Claude Swanson

Grace Tully, Jno Jennerich
and Louise Hackmeister

May 15, 1940

Dear Miss Dickerman:

I am returning your copy of the story of the President's desk, with just two minor corrections.

You will be interested to know the uproar which this desire to collect historical data caused.

The day after you left, burned matches were discovered in the waste basket and one desk drawer was found partly open. The Secret Service men were turned loose on finding the person who went near the President's desk! Everyone, including me, was finger-printed. No one was told anything about this grave concern, and so when I asked Mr. Crim to check on the accuracy of your statement, everyone was vastly relieved, including the President, who had been deeply concerned.

Mrs. Roosevelt and I are pretty firm about letting anyone go into her room to look for things, and out of respect for the other side of the house, I asked Mr. Crim to check your inscription, rather than go myself into the President's study.

These are such desperately serious times, everyone is much more watchful than ever and I imagine the Secret Service wanted to make sure that we had no one in the house who would have any interest in the contents of the President's desk. Those of us who have known the President so long I imagine find it difficult to appreciate what others like the Secret Service feel when they know how carefully the President and his papers must be guarded.

However, all's well that ends well.

Affectionately, Malvina

CHRISTMAS
1939

*I am hoping you can find some-
thing you want for the department
with*

A MERRY CHRISTMAS

from

THE PRESIDENT

and MRS. ROOSEVELT

TEMPORARY PERMIT No. 191

ADMIT BEARER

Marion Dickerman
SIGNATURE

TO HYDE PARK RESTRICTED AREA

CLASSIFICATION Commr. SEX Female RACE White

AGE 50 HT. 5'-10" WT. 165

HAIR Gray EYES Brown

PURPOSE Resident. Michael F. Reilly
SUPERVISING AGENT, U. S. SECRET SERVICE

Franklin D. Roosevelt
Vice President
FIDELITY AND DEPOSIT COMPANY OF MARYLAND
55 Liberty Street   New York City

November 18, 1925.

Dear Nan:

Many thanks for the checks. You will get another bill in a few days! Ain't it awful!

I am sending the book on Colonial Life -
a copy of the limited edition - as my first contribution
to the library!

I hear that Ralph Burnham of Ipswich, Mass has
got out a booklet of hooked rugs. Why don't you write ✓
him for it?

Wasn't that a nice 3 days we had. Only wish
you could have stayed longer.

Affectionately,

F.D.R.

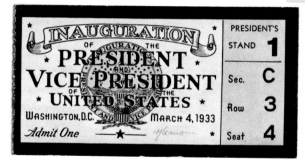

INAUGURATION
of
the
PRESIDENT
AND
VICE PRESIDENT
of
the
UNITED STATES
WASHINGTON, D.C.   MARCH 4, 1933
Admit One ─── ★ ───

PRESIDENT'S
STAND   1
Sec.   C
Row   3
Seat   4

NOT TRANSFERABLE

Miss Marian Dickerman

will please present this card at the

Picnic Grounds

𝕳𝖞𝖉𝖊 𝕻𝖆𝖗𝖐

Sunday, April 30, 1939

~~Saturday, April 29, 1939~~

at 2 o'clock

THE WHITE HOUSE
WASHINGTON

January 13, 1938

Dear Marion:

     We are having the President's birthday
dinner on the 29th of January this year at 7:30
here in the White House.

     I thought instead of making speeches
at the dinner this year, it would be amusing if
each person would come either in costume or with
something to present to the President as a reminder of some special incident, and the President
will be asked to guess what the incident is. The
other guests may join in the contest and we will
all keep score. If the President has a perfect
score, he will be given a prize. Of course if
you prefer making a speech describing your incident, or to write something to be read, or in
some way to act out the incident, that will be
fine. The ladies as usual will leave the gentlemen free after dinner for their usual entertainment.

     We are hoping very much that you and
Nancy will be able to come and are looking forward to a happy evening.

Affectionately,

Eleanor Roosevelt

Miss Dickerman

I.O.U.

*This paper knife is made from the wood in the
original roof of the White House. The Val Kill
Shop was not able to finish them in time but
they will go to you soon.*

E.R.

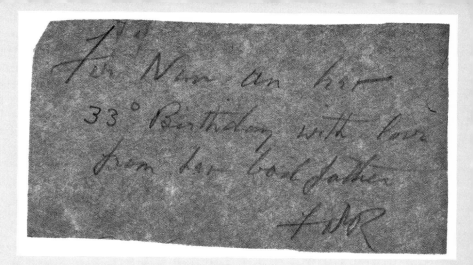

For Nina on her
33° Birthday with love
from her God father
FDR

CHRISTMAS
1935

A MERRY CHRISTMAS

from

THE PRESIDENT

and MRS. ROOSEVELT

The President and Mrs. Roosevelt

request the pleasure of the company of

Miss Dickerman

at a picnic luncheon

Sunday, June the eleventh

Hyde Park

FDR

IDR in his car especially designed for him by friend Edsel Ford. "Franklin was awfully mean to the Secret Service sometimes. He would drive off in his car down little country roads they couldn't possibly go down and across the fields at Hyde Park."

With Sistie and Anna at the pool at Val Kill.

An informal interview with newspapermen.

Celebrating a birthday for Louis Howe.

F D R

Enjoying a drink.

With Helen (Mrs. Vincent) Astor, a Dutchess County neighbor.

With Caroline O'Day.

At the "Big House" at Hyde Park.

Eleanor

Editing one of her manuscripts.

With Missy after a horseback ride.

"Eleanor and Nancy made trips in the
Buick without the Secret Service.
She loathed being followed.
Franklin gave her a pistol which
she learned to shoot. She carried it
in the car's glove compartment, and
I often wondered what advantage
it was."

At "Tivoli," on the Hudson, her
grandmother's home.

With Earl Miller at Chazy Lake.

Playing with Sistie on the White House lawn.

In her hiking attire.

With Westbrook Pegler, when he was a friend.

With Sara, on the White House steps.

"Eleanor was often teased about her constant knitting. Will Rogers once surmised, 'She was knitting in the names of future victims of the guillotine.'"

Warm Springs, 1934

INTERLUDE

OF
MEMORY
AND
HISTORY

ALL THROUGH the early formative years of their friendship, Marion, Nancy, and Eleanor had their comings and goings unusually well recorded on film. Nancy, who almost always had her camera with her, and whose use of a self-timer enabled her to be in many of the pictures she took, was an expert photographer. But it was with the settling in at the cottage that there began to accumulate the bulk of the photographs now owned and often pored over by Marion on Sunset Hill Road—the largest private and hitherto unpublished collection of still pictures of the Roosevelt family life in the world.

They are mounted for the most part in large albums bound in red leather, and for Marion each of them is not only a tangible memory in itself but also an evocation of a sliding panel of memories that moves back and forth, in and out of consciousness, with no regard for chronology. Or perhaps one had better use here the metaphor of a wheel of memory, which once the sight of a picture has given it a shove, seems to turn of its own volition and to generate as it does so its own kind of time—a time having nothing to do with the abstract linear straightforwardness of clock or calendar.

Certainly the metaphor of the wheel appears a more apt description of the tangible results and psychological effects of the picture-taking upon which Nancy embarked a year or so after the cottage became her home. In the spring of 1928 she purchased a 16-millimeter movie camera, and with her usual swift efficiency, made herself as expert in motion picture photography as she had long been with stills. Thereafter she wound time on reels, snatching from the Roosevelt years not just flat instants but long minutes, and ultimately many crowded hours, for later viewing.

To look at the albums in Marion's company, to view the motion pictures with her, watching her reactions and listening to her comments, is to be transported into a world of vivid moments having, as they present themselves, no temporal sequential order. A timeless world, a virtually eternal summer. There are a few, far-spaced glimpses of winter. Here is Marion in heavy overcoat beside a frozen Val Kill, her beloved dog Deen beside her; here she skates on the pond; here the cottage is seen across a snow-heaped yard, "looking bleak indeed"; here Eleanor and Marion ride under leafless trees in Washington's Rock Creek Park, their frozen breaths trailing behind them; and here logs in the fireplace at the cottage blaze against the cold of a winter's night. But for the most part the sun shines here warm and bright upon a summer field and wood, upon pond and stream and swimming pool, upon wide sweeps of summer lawn and the vegetables and flowers of Nancy's invariably successful gardens. Green grass grows lushly. Roses, larkspur, delphinium, daisies, and pansies bloom. Birds dart and sing as a soft wind whispers through the thick-leaved boughs of trees.

Eleanor lies, clad in white, upon a blanket on the cottage lawn, reading a manuscript. (By 1927 she, as Mrs. Franklin D. Roosevelt, had become a frequent contributor to national magazines of articles, chiefly about the role of women in private and public life.) FDR regards with stern concentration one of his hands twisting the other in a hand trick he is doing as he sits in the picnic area at Val Kill, and then, his trick completed, throws back his head with a triumphant smile. ("We had asked him a question which annoyed him and which he had no intention of answering, and this was his way of turning us off," Marion recalls, adding, "I'm not sure it wasn't something he wanted to do to our necks right then!") Nancy stands on the Roosevelt dock below the Big House, holding in her hand the boat she has made for the annual model boat race across the Hudson at Crum Elbow, an event initiated and managed by FDR and Howe. (". . . there was always a great deal of secrecy for weeks before the race concerning the wood being used, the height of the masts, the keel shapes, and so on, of the boats being entered," Marion remembers, "—and the winner was awarded a silver cup by Franklin.") FDR sits with Missy at the edge of the Val Kill pool, both in swimsuits, he dangling his withered legs and she her shapely ones in the water while Eleanor stands in swimsuit above them, all of them gazing in rapt, smiling attention at something going on across the pool. (Once, sitting beside the pool with FDR, Marion deliberately brushed with a blade of grass the bottom of his bare foot and exclaimed in surprise, "It moved!" She was at once abashed, even a little fearful—a fact indicative of the essential privacy he maintained and the personal authority he exerted, for all his seeming open frankness, friendliness, and total lack of pretension. His reply was a matter-of-fact statement that people were mistaken who believed a paralyzed limb could have no feeling, that because the motor nerves were dead or injured the sympathetic nerves must also be. "Not so!" he said, with emphasis and a rueful shake of his head. "I didn't close my eyes until three o'clock this morning . . ." And this, says Marion, was "the only direct reference I ever heard him make to his affliction. I was so ashamed!")

A middle-aged woman of broad and plain but pleasant countenance, wearing a voluminous long skirt, feeds turkeys within a fenced enclosure. ("Nellie Johannesen came to take charge of the weaving when we added this to Val-Kill Industries," Marion explains. "She had two sons who worked under Nan in the shop. She was a Swedish woman— a wonderful earthly peasant type who took wonderful care of us and always wanted lots of animals. She had a dozen turkeys each year, and when it rained she'd rush out and spread her skirts, which had yards of cloth in them, and get the turkeys to stand underneath, because she had heard that a turkey must never be allowed to get its feet wet. But she wasn't a bit squeamish about killing and eating them. Eleanor was! One year we ate the eleventh turkey for Thanksgiving and planned to have the twelfth for Christmas, but then the twelfth one died—of heartache, I do believe, being all alone.") FDR, in a chair beside Val Kill pond, celebrating his namesake son's twentieth birthday, watches with a smile, then laughs uproariously, as all four of his sons cavort on the pond in a canoe, finally capsizing it and casting themselves into the water. He is the center of a family group. Marion and Eleanor (Nancy handled the movie camera), Anna and James's pretty, vivacious young wife, Betsy (she was the daughter of the famous Boston brain surgeon, Harvey Cushing), are among those sitting and standing on the grass around him. And they all smile with delight, and laugh, too, as they watch. All, that is, save Marion. Her face is mournful. "It was my canoe," she explains, "and they did it no good. As a matter of fact it was never afterward the same again."

There are interior shots also.

Here is Nan at her drafting table in the shop, Eleanor standing above her, and here is Nan by herself in the finishing room. Here is the cottage living room, empty of people but obviously much lived in, with books and magazines scattered over one drop-leaf Val-Kill table and on the corners of a davenport facing the fieldstone fireplace, as well as on a round table beside a lounge chair. There are papers piled on the Val-Kill desk in the corner, beside which is an upright typewriter with a sheet of paper in its roller. A cluttered, pleasant room. Hanging on the wall is a framed naval print that was presented to Nan and Marion by FDR, a collector of such prints. Here is another view of the living room as seen from the corner where the typewriter stands, showing the staircase to the cottage's second floor, where the three friends shared a large bedroom. Above the drop-leaf table hangs a pewter chandelier designed and made by Nancy.

Here is the library of the Big House, also empty of people as we view it, but richly peopled in Marion's memory. She sees in her mind's eye, she hears with memory's ear, the after-dinner gatherings before the fireplace—Granny, Nancy, Marion herself, often Caroline O'Day, often some of the Roosevelt children—with Eleanor's knitting needles clicking now and then as FDR tells a funny story, generally out of his own experience; or with FDR and the others listening while Eleanor reads aloud; or with everyone engaged in animated talk, expressing strong and often contradictory opinions about manners and morals and public affairs.

In the library, opposite the place on the davenport where—we are told—Eleanor habitually sits, are two very special articles of furniture.

Marion points to them.

"The 'Governor's chairs,' " she says, explaining that New York State gave one to FDR for his first term as governor, the other for his second.

And as she does so we are jarred out of the timeless summer world of Marion's memories into the flowing world of "before" and "after," of "now" and "then"—the world of history, which not only imposes a dated temporal order upon these otherwise helter-skelter images but also imparts a public interest to what would otherwise be home movies and family albums of no particular interest to anyone save those pictured in them or their friends and relatives.

We might in any case have regarded with a mild, compassionate curiosity this big, handsome, laughing, swimsuited man whose physical appearance is, overall, a contradiction in itself, being shockingly weak in his lower limbs, though magnificently strong and healthy above them; but we *do* regard him with a certain fascination, seeing him as physically symbolic of the American Republic in the twentieth century—so immensely powerful in some ways, so ghastly feeble in others—because we know that he was a central focus of history through twelve years of unparalleled world crisis.

We probably would take no interest at all in Eleanor, as we see her in one of Nancy's movie sequences, standing beside Val Kill's outdoor fireplace, were we wholly lacking in historical and biographical information about her. She appears dull and commonplace as she stands there—a tall, plainly dressed woman whose unsmiling face, as she wipes potato salad from her chin, is devoid of charm. That we *do* watch her with more than interest is due to our sense, derived from historical context, that this gesture we see her make is but one of myriads of fun-flecked gestures by which she removed from her hurt, strained spirit impediments to its full growth and flowering.

What we witness here, then, in this summer world of sunshine and laughter and picnics, are events of no small historic importance, however trivial of themselves alone. Or perhaps one should say that their importance actually consists of their casual triviality, since they constitute in sum the recreative process, the means of a renewal of the self and a restoration of depleted energies of mind and body, whereby this man was enabled to withstand for a dozen years pressures of history that would have crushed most men within a few months, and whereby this woman grew to the independent greatness that was hers (millions deemed her "First Lady of the World") after her husband's death.

PART TWO

THE MORTALITY OF FRIENDSHIP

S I X

ELEANOR was tense, fearful of not doing well, when she met her first Todhunter classes in American history and English and American literature, taught to older girls, in September 1927. Leaning heavily upon Marion's experienced counsel, gratefully accepting Marion's encouragement and praise, which were sincere (as a teacher Eleanor was "a natural," Marion thought), she continued to be nagged by doubts about her abilities. And these doubts were not removed by the depressing results of the examinations she gave at the end of her first semester.

"I can't say I am set up by the exams my children did," she wrote her husband, in typical understatement, on February 2, 1928. "I only flunked one but the others were none too good."

From the first, however, she had no doubts at all about the kind of teacher she *wanted* to be, the kind of teaching she *wanted* to do.

When she was asked by Eunice Fuller Barnard, education editor of the *New York Times*, in an interview published in 1932, how it happened she had taken up teaching so late in life, Eleanor "turned to the calm-browed woman who sat opposite her at the principal's desk" and replied that "the first reason is Miss Dickerman here"; the second "was my admiration for my old teacher, Mlle. Souvestre." She went on to explain that Mlle. Souvestre "provided my first intimate contact with a great personality. . . . It was the time of the Boer War and she was intensely pro-Boer. The debate as to whether that war was right or wrong gave me my first burning concern with a grave public issue. The main thing in education, I have always since thought, is the interest aroused in a young mind by a stimulating, vivid personality."

But Eleanor did not carry this "cult of personality" too far. To inspire was not by itself enough, and specific subject matter must be learned. As regards the latter operation, Eleanor subscribed, wrote Mrs. Barnard, "to the modern theory that one should start with young people's present interests and lead them into an enlivened understanding of every possible phase of the world into which they are going." The process of learning was one of relating oneself to an ever-enlarging environment, from which, by means of truly vital working connections, the self derived the materials for continuous growth. Said Eleanor to her interviewer: "It is the teacher's function to manage this relating process, to seize all opportunities, however unpromising, to make all history and literature and the seemingly barren study of the machinery of government somehow akin to the things the pupils are doing in their daily life."

The course in current affairs that she was teaching in 1932 was entitled "Happenings," and was taught in an informal discussion group, with assigned readings in current periodicals. There was, for this class, no textbook. ". . . we try as far as possible to give the girls vivid, first-hand experiences, . . ." Eleanor explained. "We take them to see Ellis Island and model tenements, for example, instead of merely reading about them." Yet there was in the conduct of this Todhunter class, as of all others, a rigid core of discipline. ". . . we still have frequent tests, and mid-term and final examinations, as well as the reports and marks of the traditional school." Marion insisted on this; Eleanor concurred. "For we believe that the girls will have to take certain hurdles in life, and that hurdles in school are an important preparation. We try, however, not to compare one child with another. And each girl plots a graph of her own term marks to demonstrate to herself whether she is gaining or losing."

Each school-day morning the hundred uniformed Todhunter girls marched, on low-heeled oxfords, to the sound of martial piano music, to the long assembly hall, there to be greeted by principal and—on three days a week—associate principal, "stately figures in tailored dark red gowns," as Mrs. Barnard described them. The program started with the School Prayer: "O God, give us clean hands, clean words, clean thoughts. Help us to stand for the hard right against the easy wrong. Save us from habits that harm. Teach us to work as hard and play as fair, in Thy sight alone, as though all the world saw us. Keep us ready to help others and send us chances every day to do a little good and so grow more like Christ. Amen."

In general it was acknowledged between Eleanor and Marion that, though Eleanor was inclined to stress the progressive and Marion the traditional in education, the overall balance thus achieved was in every respect fortunate for the school. Eleanor knew that it was by the time her second semester of teaching, which went much better than her first, came to an end.

By then, she, Nancy, and Marion owned the school jointly—though Nancy, her time and energy fully engaged by her job with the State Democratic Committee and her management of Val-Kill Industries, took no active part in the enterprise. Eleanor's own part was curtailed by her other commitments—she could devote only two and one-half to three days a week to teaching—but it was the most richly rewarding occupation in which she had ever engaged, as she said over and over again to Marion, gratefully. Through Todhunter she was achieving a truly definite identity, wholly apart from her relationship with Franklin, in the service and shadow of whose immense ambition she had to

79

operate politically, and even from her relationship with Marion and Nan.

In all the major projects in which the three friends had joined thus far, hers had been a subordinate part. The designing and building of Val Kill Cottage, the landscaping of its grounds, had been predominantly Nan's (and Franklin's) enterprise. Val-Kill Industries was largely Nan's conception and predominantly hers in execution. The cottage itself remained Nan's and Marion's home, primarily. And the *Women's Democratic News*, originally suggested by Howe, gave severely limited opportunity for individual expression. In a Todhunter classroom, however, Eleanor was the dominant figure, doing something she loved to do and knew she did well. She had gained a profession and professional standing in terms of which she could clearly define herself: she could say with truth and conviction that she was an educator.

Marion is certain that Eleanor would have "loved to go" to the 1928 Democratic National Convention when it assembled in late June in Houston, Texas, despite Eleanor's assertion in *This I Remember*, published twenty-one years later, that she "had no desire to take part in the hurly-burly of a convention. . . ."

FDR was to be a major star of the big show—in 1928 as in 1924, he was to make the speech nominating Al Smith for the Presidency—and was taking Elliott as aide. Father and son were in Warm Springs in mid-June, practicing hour after hour for FDR's physical appearance before the public, for FDR was determined to show himself this time as a man merely lame, not crippled. ("I told everyone at that State Committee meeting yesterday that you were going to Houston without crutches!" Eleanor had written him in April.) With his left hand grasping Elliott's arm, a cane in his right hand, he would *walk* across the stage. And there to see him do it would be Caroline O'Day, who was going as a delegate; Marion, who was Caroline's alternate; and Nancy, who was going as a member of the delegation staff.

80

Granny had sailed for Europe, taking James with her. Eleanor, with Franklin, Jr., and John, was left alone as mistress of the Big House at Hyde Park, and disliking it intensely. ". . . it is horrid, rainy weather and I am quite unreasonably depressed," she wrote her husband on June 22, "partly because I feel uncomfortable about servants. . . ." She would be listening to his speech on the radio, she said, and would "expire if it doesn't work!" An hour or so later she went to Hyde Park's railway station to say good-bye to Marion, and to Elinor and Henry Morgenthau, and Marion remembers how forlorn she looked, standing on the platform in the rain, waving, as the train pulled out.

When Marion returned from Houston, Eleanor was eager for eye-witness accounts of the proceedings there. The great moment, as she already knew (her radio had worked perfectly), had come when FDR made his nominating speech. Eleanor and Marion had both feared that this address would not measure up to his "Happy Warrior" effort, but if anything his personal triumph surpassed that of 1924. Moreover, its specific aim had this time been achieved: Alfred E. Smith was the Democratic nominee for President of the United States, running against Republican Herbert Hoover.

In the presidential election campaign itself, that year, Eleanor took a far more active part than her husband. FDR was displeased by Smith's choice of John J. Raskob as chairman of the Democratic National Committee and ex officio manager of the presidential campaign. Like Smith, Raskob was a fervent Roman Catholic, which was bound to encourage a concentration by anti-Catholics upon the "phony issue," as FDR called it, of "religion." Like Smith, Raskob was a leading opponent of Prohibition, which meant concentration upon another "phony issue," in FDR's view, that of "wet vs. dry." (Eleanor strongly favored Prohibition, but thought other issues more important.) Worst of all, in FDR's opinion, Raskob was a big businessman—chairman of the finance committee of General Motors; vice-president of E. I. Du-Pont de Nemours. This meant that his appointment, and the kind of campaign he ran, would blot out the basic issue, that of Democratic liberalism vs. Republican conservatism, or democracy vs. business oligarchy, upon which, FDR believed, the presidential campaign *ought* to be waged.

With these strictures Eleanor agreed. Nevertheless, while FDR "did not feel he could do a great deal of work in the campaign" and only "came to the office occasionally," having "assigned Louis Howe to represent him . . . full-time" at headquarters, as Eleanor wrote, she herself dedicated to Smith's battle a truly awesome energy (". . . I was still fairly young and could put in prodigious hours of work . . .") —as if determined to extract the last full measure of personal experience from political activity before it was denied her. (She was convinced, as was FDR in 1928, that all overt political activity on her part had to cease when he won elective office.) And her commitment to Smith grew with the energy, the hard work she invested in his campaign—grew also in proportion to her revulsion against the viciously bigoted and scurrilous campaign waged by his opponents.

When school opened in September, however, Eleanor maintained in full force her working connection with Todhunter. On her teaching days she was at Todhunter from 8:30 in the morning until noon, then went to Democratic headquarters, where, as she recalled later, "I stayed until the work was finished at night, often well after midnight." Working with her there was her personal secretary, Miss Malvina (Tommy) Thompson, who had formerly been Marion's secretary, and Miss Grace Tully who, having formerly been Cardinal Hayes's secretary, became later Missy LeHand's assistant and successor as secretary to FDR. When Eleanor managed to get away to the Big House or the cottage for a weekend, she worked upon letters and documents unremittingly.

And as if this were not enough, she permitted herself to be persuaded to go with Nancy to the state Democratic convention in Rochester on October 1. The fact, in its circumstantial context, is significant of a tangled, self-contradictory motivation in Eleanor at that point.

Ever since Smith's presidential nomination, great and growing pressures had been put upon FDR to run for Governor. He was the strongest of all the Democrats who might run; and the strongest possible state ticket was needed to help Smith carry New York, without whose electoral votes he could not defeat Hoover. But the Warm Springs enterprise required all the time and energy FDR could devote to it. He still believed, if with reduced conviction, that his own concentrated use of Warm Springs' facilities would enable him to throw away his braces in another year or two. And he and Howe were privately convinced, in part by the kind of campaign Raskob was managing, that 1928 was not a good year for the Democrats nationally and that, in New York, the Democratic gubernatorial candidate could well go down to defeat. In any case, according to Howe's time schedule, FDR was not to run again for office until 1932; he was scheduled to win the governorship that year, win reelection in 1934, win the White House in 1936. For these reasons FDR, with Howe, was determined to resist the pressures from the Smith camp to the end. Hence his departure from Hyde Park for Warm Springs in mid-September.

Of all this, Eleanor was aware, and she also knew that Smith and his associates desired her presence in Rochester primarily so that they could press her to press her husband to accept the nomination. "I have to go, . . ." she wrote her husband on September 30, "but I wish I didn't . . . for everyone makes me so uncomfortable. They feel so strongly about your running and even good explanations can be made to sound foolish." But *why* did she "have to go"? Was it wholly impossible for her to justify staying away? ("Even though I was teaching school and working in the national campaign headquarters . . . I attended the . . . convention . . . that fall," she writes in *This I Remember*, as if she went *despite* obstacles to her doing so.) The questions dangle, unanswered.

All we know is the story Marion later heard from Eleanor's lips, a stripped factual account, and in somewhat more detail from Nancy, who was present with Eleanor at most of the meetings on October 1 in Rochester's Hotel Seneca. Eleanor arrived at the hotel almost simultaneously with Al Smith, and soon thereafter she was summoned to conference with him and his closest associates. They showed her a long telegram just received from Warm Springs, in which FDR again refused to run and laid heavy stress upon the health reasons for his refusal. Did it state *all* his reasons for not running? She knew of no others. Raskob "asked whether it would have any effect upon Franklin's decision if he were relieved of all financial anxieties." She was "sure it would not." They urged her to call him and talk about it. She refused. They tried to call him themselves, were unable to reach him (he had arranged an all-day picnic for the express purpose of making himself unavailable), became convinced that he would refuse to accept any calls from them, and finally, late in the evening, begged Eleanor to place a person-to-person call to him. Surely he would accept a call from his wife! All she had to do, said Smith, was say "hello" and then turn the phone over to him.

She hesitated for a long moment, during which everyone in the room silently, intently watched her.

She knew, as Nancy knew, that the mere fact of her placing such a call would mean to her husband that she was on Smith's side—that she felt he, FDR, *ought* to accept the nomination. But at last she did as Smith wished: she got her husband on the phone, and as soon as he had answered, handed the phone to Al Smith.

Then she fled.

". . . I hurried from the room to gather up my belongings and catch the train for New York City," she wrote in her memoirs, because she had to teach a nine o'clock class at Todhunter next morning. And it was not until next morning when, at Grand Central Station, she bought a newspaper, that she knew her husband had finally yielded to the Smith-Raskob importunities and would by noon of October 2 be named the Democratic candidate for Governor of New York. She showed no particular excitement, no particular emotion at all, over this when she arrived at Todhunter, as Marion remembers.* "I sometimes

* In *This I Remember*, Eleanor writes that she boarded the train "with Miss Dickerman" who "had come up to the convention with Miss Cook to help with any work the women's division . . . might have." Actually, Marion's Todhunter duties kept her from attending the convention.

wonder whether I really wanted Franklin to run," she wrote twenty years later. She took no active part whatever in her husband's gubernatorial campaign; she continued to devote all her energies, save those Todhunter absorbed, to Smith's presidential campaign; and when her husband won while Smith lost she showed slight joy over the former event while expressing great grief over the latter. "No, I am not excited about my husband's election," she blurted out to one reporter. "I don't care. What difference can it make to me?" Since "the rest of the ticket didn't get in, what does it matter?"

Marion has sharp memories of Eleanor's regrets, openly confessed to her bosom friends on the morrow of the election, over what must now be the giving up of the political and civic organizational activities she had greatly enjoyed. She resigned from the Democratic State Committee and from the boards of such organizations as the Women's Trade Union League, which lobbied for special legislation in Albany. She ceased making political speeches, and for a time, on her husband's orders, declined invitations to attend purely political gatherings. Her name appeared for the last time as editor of the *Women's Democratic News* in the December 1928 issue (Caroline O'Day was thereafter listed as editor). But she simultaneously made it crystal clear that she would *not* become merely "the Governor's wife," presiding over the huge, towered and turreted Executive Mansion.

When she visited Albany in December, as a guest of the Smiths, to arrange for moving the Roosevelts into the mansion, she chose as her husband's bedroom a large, sunny corner room on the second floor; assigned to Missy another large bedroom down the hall on the same floor; and chose for herself a smaller back bedroom, as if to emphasize that she considered her "first lady" duties to be less important than others she performed in her own right, as Eleanor Roosevelt. With social secretary and mansion servants she planned a weekly schedule. Each Sunday evening during the school year she would take the night train down to New York City, where she would meet her classes at Todhunter on Mondays and Tuesdays, and Wednesday mornings.

She would take the noon train back on Wednesday, arriving at the mansion in time for her official "at home," from 4:30 to 6:00 P.M.

Thus she determined the pattern whereby she used her Todhunter connection as a means, actually her principal single means, of maintaining her independent identity against the threat of being utterly blotted out by the growing power and glory of FDR. And she managed to weave her multifarious obligations, interests, and activities together in a way that made each of them reinforce and profit from the others, while all of them together enlarged and enriched her personal life, her human selfhood—an amazing feat. It required an immense and highly disciplined energy. It required iron self-control, directed by a hard and sharp intelligence. It required a rare conception of overall pattern and ultimate goals, and an almost frightening willpower. Having divided each of her days into definitely assigned segments of time, she must shift her concentrated attention swiftly, smoothly, from the thing that had occupied one segment to the often totally different thing that occupied the next. And the center or core of the pattern she wove was the Todhunter School.

In a sense and to a degree, she made Albany's Executive Mansion and legislative halls a laboratory extension of the school, exploiting to the full the opportunity to make politics and government an exciting human enterprise for her students. A Todhunter class came at Eleanor's and FDR's invitation to the Governor's inauguration in January 1929. A Todhunter class was again present at FDR's second gubernatorial inauguration in January 1931, after he had won reelection by an unprecedentedly huge majority and thereby became, amid deepening economic depression, the leading contender for the Democratic presidential nomination in 1932. She had her students as guests in the mansion on other occasions, and she and Marion used her authority and prestige to attract speakers of national repute for special Todhunter exercises. In June of 1932 the commencement speaker was Franklin D. Roosevelt himself; his address, delivered only a few weeks before that year's Democratic National Convention, received national attention, augmenting Todhunter's fame.

86

"I like it [teaching] better than anything else I do," said Eleanor in response to a question from Mrs. Barnard in the 1932 *New York Times Magazine.*

"But when you are in the White House, I suppose, you must give it up," said Mrs. Barnard.

"No, indeed; even then I shall keep my connection as associate principal and part owner of this school. I shall help in the supervision of the courses and in other problems as they may arise. I hope to run up here at least every two weeks. Perhaps, if I can manage it, I may even attend the opening exercises once a week. And I shall have the older girls at the White House occasionally, as I have been having them at the Executive Mansion in Albany."

SEVEN

WHEN the Roosevelts moved into the Executive Mansion in Albany in 1929, the post of the Governor's personal bodyguard went to a husky New York City policeman named Gus Gennerich. Gennerich was replacing a Corporal Earl Miller, who had been Al Smith's bodyguard during Smith's last two terms and who was now reassigned to be personal aide and bodyguard to the Governor's lady.

Young Miller, famous throughout the state police barracks for his attractiveness to, and attraction toward, the "fair sex," was a handsome, dashing figure of a man. Possessor of a magnificent physique, he had been a circus acrobat, a champion amateur welterweight boxer; had taught boxing and judo at the State Police School; had won many cups for his horsemanship at state and county fairs. He was also a man of generous emotions and an instinctive if sometimes crudely expressed courtesy. His had been a rough life, emotionally as well as physically:

88

he had been orphaned at age twelve, had served a hitch in the navy, had been unhappily married and acrimoniously divorced.

From the first, his admiration for Eleanor was immense and openly shown. Soon there developed between the two a rare friendship, having in it elements of maternal and filial devotion (he came to her with his personal problems; she advised him, mothered him) along with elements of romantic gallantry (he, a most masculine man, deferred to her and protected her in a way that made her feel, as she had not felt for a dozen years, a very feminine woman). He became, within a short time, part of the intimate family circle.

While others of the mansion's state police detail ate in the kitchen, Earl Miller dined at the Roosevelt table. At teas presided over by Eleanor in the mansion, Earl Miller was invariably present. When Eleanor traveled, Earl Miller accompanied her, often as her sole companion. And the two exchanged frequent gifts, with Eleanor sometimes making rather ostentatious display of his gifts to her. (For instance, he once gave her a three-foot-high metal plaque of a pickaninny eating a watermelon—a strange gift to one famous for her commitment to full racial equality; she had it mounted on the chimney of the fireplace in the Val Kill picnic area.) Inevitably, all this provoked a certain amount of snide comment. Granny, for one, expressed displeasure that "Corporal" Miller, whose place had been in the servants' hall, was now "Mister" Miller, whom she must entertain as a guest. As for FDR, he simply accepted the state trooper as one of the family entourage— blandly, cheerfully, indifferently.

Yet Earl Miller served for Eleanor a useful purpose aside from, but in conjunction with, her human relationship with him. He put her at ease. When she was asked to pose for news photographers, something she had always dreaded to do and showed that she dreaded, he encouraged her relaxation by making jokes as the cameras snapped. Her published appearance was considerably improved. He encouraged her to ride more, for fun and exercise, and obtained for her the horse "Dot," which was precisely suited to her temperament and level of skill as horsewoman and which, because it was hers, became nationally known after she was in the White House. (He persuaded FDR as Governor to try riding, too—a sport FDR had greatly enjoyed before his polio—but the experiment, made at Warm Springs, failed because FDR could not clasp a horse's flanks between his legs.) He also encouraged her to drive more in her car, instead of letting others take the wheel, insisting that she was intrinsically "a good driver" and that the minor accidents she had had could "have happened to anybody."

In general, Earl Miller became a major one of the vital forces or influences whereby Eleanor gained steadily in self-confidence and emotional balance during the years of FDR's governorship and presidential candidacy and, indeed, through the early years of his Presidency.

This influence had not yet had much effect when, in the spring of 1929, at FDR's initial suggestion, plans were made for Eleanor, with Marion and Nancy, to take the soon-to-be fifteen-year-old Franklin, Jr., and thirteen-year-old John on a European tour. The weaving together into a coherent, mutually reinforcing pattern of the various strands of Eleanor's life as Governor's wife had barely begun at that time, but was sufficiently advanced to cause her to wonder if she really wanted to go to Europe right then, leaving the "thick of things" for weeks on end.

With Nancy and Marion, she had already discovered that, in giving up her official posts in the Women's Division and civic organizations in order to conform to the position imposed by her husband's election, she had sacrificed nothing of real power and influence in public affairs—had, in fact, gained greatly in these. By inviting her civic organizational friends to the mansion, she and they could often accomplish more in a few pleasant minutes with FDR at tea or dinner than could have been done in hard weeks of legislative lobbying. Especially was this so after FDR, soon following his inauguration, relaxed his rule against her participation in public political meetings, provided that she herself made no overtly political speeches. In early April she presided over, and thereby gained publicity for, a Women's Trade Union League luncheon at which the five-day work week for women was promoted. A month later, at Granny's somewhat surprising invitation, a large Trade Union League celebration was held at the Big House in Hyde Park, to mark the paying off of the mortgage on the league club house, for which Eleanor had helped to raise money; at this affair Eleanor was able to present the Governor himself as, in her words, "the *pièce de résistance*." ("Franklin was absolutely charming, of course," Marion says, "and the league girls were simply devastated by him. They went away singing his praises in almost worshipful tones.")

And FDR profited politically, as he astutely aimed to do, from his wife's much-publicized liberalism. Marion stresses this. She stresses, too, her own conviction that FDR was as much an idealist as Eleanor was, fundamentally. But he was also a politician, and as such he was more than willing to have Eleanor attract and help him to hold the liberal vote while he, when he deemed it expedient, took a conservative position. If some of her activities brought right-wingers raging into his office he could point out that his "missus" had, after all, a strong mind and will of her own. Never, however, as Marion points out, did he flatly contradict or disown Eleanor's liberalism. Always he indicated, at least tacitly, that he and his wife were truly a team, that they pulled in tandem toward the same ultimate goals.

Eleanor of course confessed to Marion and Nancy her ambivalent emotions about the European trip: "I want to go, yet don't want to leave." She was not only reluctant to be "out of touch" with the exciting goings-on in New York for so long a period, she also felt that the trip would be a "fearful effort." She worried that she, Nancy, and Marion might not be able to cope with the rambunctious energies of two teen-aged boys. She worried about the cost of the trip; for while FDR's personal income was now sharply reduced (his salary as Governor was meager compared to that paid him by Van Lear Black's company), his expenses were as sharply increased, being boosted that spring by sizable doctors' bills for various ailments and accidental injuries sustained by each of the four boys. ("Eleanor wrote me afterward that her share of the profits which we all had had from Tod-

hunter helped to make the trip possible for her," says Marion.) But
there was never any real doubt that the trip would be made. FDR was
quite insistent upon it: he particularly wanted the boys to tour the
battlefields he had seen in France in the summer of 1918.

And as May gave way to June, the three friends shaped a plan that,
echoing the trips they had made in earlier summers, greatly enhanced
their pleasurable anticipation of this one. They decided that they would
take with them two touring cars—the Buick that Nancy and Marion
then owned, and Eleanor's Chevrolet. This would not only enable them
to go their separate ways on days when some of them wanted to do one
thing, others another; it would also enable them to carry with them
their camping paraphernalia. For—and this was the most exciting part
of their plan—they intended to camp out in England and across the
Continent as they had camped out in New York and across New
England in other years. The two boys were, naturally, enthusiastic at
the prospect and, says Marion, "the Governor agreed, for he thought
we were perfectly capable."

But when Granny heard about it she was at once, Marion goes on,
"bitterly opposed." She questioned the "capabilities" of the three
women "as chauffeurs" in Europe and in the British Isles. But "more
fundamentally," she "felt that the Governor's wife and two sons should
not visit Europe in such an informal manner." She said so incisively,
emphatically.

Nevertheless, buoyed up by what she believed to be the two boys'
enthusiasm, Eleanor persisted with the plan. Until, as Marion puts it,
"an unfortunate thing occurred."

It was during a Sunday evening supper in late June, in the dining
room of the Big House, with Granny sitting as always at the head of
the table and her son at its foot, and with Eleanor, Marion, Nancy,
Brother, John, and Elliott seated at its sides. The talk turned to the
forthcoming trip—a sad turning, for Granny seized the opportunity to
"again express her emphatic disapproval of our plans." Her views in
this matter were insulting to Eleanor, impugning as they did her good
taste, her practical judgment, and the manner of their expression did

nothing to reduce the insult. Eleanor stiffened; she looked toward her husband, no doubt for a word of support. None came. He seemed blandly unaware that anything was wrong (he generally seemed so on such occasions; he hated to take sides), though Marion and Nancy could feel the tension mounting between wife and mother-in-law.

Then, at the worst possible moment for it, Brother ventured "a wisecrack, as he sometimes innocently did," according to Marion. He opined that "Mom" would "probably land us all in the first ditch," going on to refer cheerfully to an occasion, some time ago, when she had driven them into one of the stone gateposts at the foot of the Big House drive. The icy silence that followed this sally caused the boy to realize, too late, that he trod a field laden with mines. He sought to retreat. "But I'm sure we'll be all right," he concluded lamely.

Eleanor placed her napkin on the table.

"Very well," she said to Granny, her voice quavering into high key, as it always did when she was emotional, "I will see that your grandsons travel in the way in which you think they should be accustomed."

She left the room.

It was one of those moments when FDR most bitterly regretted the loss of his legs, says Marion; for his powerful instinct was to rise and follow his hurt wife. Instead, he sternly ordered Brother to do so. The son found his mother weeping, made abject apologies ("I was only kidding"), and finally persuaded her to return to the dining room. He tried also to persuade her to carry on with the trip as planned, but in this he failed. "Eleanor could be hard," says Marion. "She used to say to us that she could forgive but not forget, and I know she *tried* to forgive, but hers was not a forgiving nature, really. In this case she was adamant. She said Nan and I could take our Buick, but she would rent cars and hire drivers—and that is what she did. She rented quite elaborate cars with chauffeurs—a Daimler in England, as I remember—at greater expense than she could afford, and insisted on the two boys, properly dressed, riding discreetly in the back seats. The boys didn't like traveling in this manner at all, of course. And Nan and I were deprived of some of the pleasure we had anticipated."

Yet most of Marion's memories of this journey are pleasant ones.

In England they saw the Lake District, Stratford-on-Avon, Stonehenge, Salisbury, Winchester, Oxford, and Hampton Court, and spent several days in London, where Nan and Marion introduced Eleanor to their friend from Endell Street Hospital days, Helena Hirst, wife of Francis Hirst, editor of *The Economist*. Eleanor and Helena Hirst subsequently became fast friends. (Two years later, after FDR was clearly established as front runner for the Democratic presidential nomination, the Hirsts came to America, and were invited by their friends the Herbert Hoovers to stay in the White House. Both the Hirsts were "steeped in history," which added to their enjoyment, but Helena "had no conception whatever of American politics," according to Marion. When she said good-bye to the Hoovers, having thanked "Herbert" for "one of the great experiences of our lives," she added the hope that "when we come back, if you're not here, the Franklin Roosevelts will be.") On the Continent, they drove through Belgium into the German Rhineland, taking a small steamer up the Rhine from Coblenz to Bingen and then back to Coblenz, where they stayed the night.

Next day was Brother's fifteenth birthday, "and he asked his mother if, as a birthday gift, he might ride with me in the Buick." Marion was delighted by this. She had a closer rapport with the boy Franklin than with any of the other Roosevelt offspring. (She vividly remembers a Saturday at the cottage when Brother was twelve or so and definite plans had been made for an after-luncheon expedition. John appeared for lunch at the proper time. Franklin, Jr., appeared not at all. And after lunch an annoyed Eleanor said they would carry out their program anyway. Marion "had a feeling," however, and said she'd remain behind "and see when Brother comes." He came bursting into the cottage at three o'clock or so. He'd been "up at the barn" with Moses Smith [the Roosevelt tenant farmer] he explained, "and the cow had a calf and I just had to stay and see it." He looked up at Marion. "Do babies come into the world the same way?" he asked. "Pretty much," said Marion. The boy shook his head thoughtfully. "Gee!" said he. "A fellow owes his mother an awful lot, doesn't he?") Marion indicated to

Eleanor, therefore, that the birthday gift Brother was asking for would be a gift to her, Marion, also. Eleanor said nothing for a long moment. Then, at last, she relented.

And Marion recalls that birthday of Brother's as one of the most pleasurable days in her own life. She and the boy had the Buick to themselves, Nan having joined Eleanor and John in the hired limousine, and they rode with the car's top down, wind and sunlight upon their tanning faces, along the narrow, winding, hill-walled valley of the Moselle. They talked, they laughed, they thoroughly enjoyed each other's company as lovely vistas of hill and field and wood, enriched by history and by a golden, almost autumnal light, shifted and turned with their turnings. They came in the late afternoon to the city of Luxembourg. There a birthday dinner was given Brother, with toasts drunk to him in champagne.

Came then the portion of the trip on which FDR had laid greatest stress.

They drove down into northern France and across the Meuse-Argonne battlefield of 1918. They stopped at Verdun, saw the great monument there inscribed "They Shall Not Pass," and visited the underground fortifications with their hundreds of rooms, their miles of passageways, where many thousands of men had lived cramped lives for weeks at a time while shells churned the earth above them, and where FDR himself had spent an almost sleepless night eleven years before. Then they went on across some of the bloodiest killing ground of the war to Belleau Wood and Château-Thierry. The two boys were particularly impressed by the huge war cemeteries, the seemingly endless rows of white crosses, and by the fact they saw only boys and old men working in the fields. (". . . there don't seem to be any men of father's age," noted Franklin, Jr.)

Subdued by what they had seen, they slanted down along the Marne through red evening light into Paris, where, as Eleanor records, they "encountered some of the hottest weather I have ever known." Despite the heat, they engaged in arduous sight-seeing, and a few days later they stopped at Chartres where, while Nan took the two boys to a cattle show, Marion and Eleanor spent richly meaningful hours at the cathedral, "remembering well parts of Henry Adams' *Mont-Saint-Michel and Chartres*, which we had read at Campo," as Marion recalls. On the day after that they visited Mont-Saint-Michel, where "we found the 'Church Militant,' a tiny island crowned by a chapel. We walked up the fascinating little streets to the very top and looked over sands which seemed to stretch to infinity. Then the tide started coming in." Marion stayed there while the others went to dinner; the sun went down and a full moon rose. The beauty was breathtaking. "I found a man with a boat, gathered the others, and he took us around the island. We were all hushed. It was overwhelming—a religious experience."

But Eleanor in her memoirs remembers Mont-Saint-Michel primarily as "the scene of one of the most violent roughhouse battles between Brother and John." There had been a good many of these. "In every city where we stayed, we climbed bell towers, and I tried to walk my sons in the evenings," writes Eleanor. "I wanted them to be so weary that they would not start roughhousing before they went to bed, since roughhousing usually turned into a battle royal. . . . I realized that I was a poor person to be taking on a trip two youngsters who needed good, hard physical exercise daily, and many times I wrote my husband how glad I should be to get home. . . ." Marion doubted that the quarrels would have been quite so frequent or violent if Eleanor had taken a different attitude toward the boys—if, for instance, she had not forced them to travel as Granny thought they should, but had instead permitted them to be "natural." For the most part, the squabbles that Eleanor took so seriously seemed to Marion "about par for the course, considering the boys' ages."

The travelers sailed for home from Cherbourg aboard the *Belgenland*, arriving in New York on September 15. "On landing," wrote Eleanor in *This I Remember*, "I breathed a sigh of relief and made a vow that never again would I take a trip in which I had to be responsible for the young."

EIGHT

M A R I O N spent little time in the Executive Mansion in Albany. During the school year, when she and Nan came up to the cottage on weekends and holidays, the Roosevelts were often at the Big House, for they found the mansion "rather austere" and got away whenever they could. And in the summers the Roosevelts lived mostly at Hyde Park.

Marion paid one visit to the mansion, however, which she will never forget.

It was in early June of 1932, halfway through the third year of the Great Depression.

In Central Park was a pitiful collection of shacks fashioned out of corrugated iron, used lumber, packing boxes, and flattened tin cans, one of several dozen so-called Hoovervilles in the New York City area, where men unable to find work huddled miserably, many of them with wives and children, in the heart of the supposedly richest city in the world. ("Running a school and serving meals, there is bound to be some waste," says Marion, "so every evening Molly Goodwin and I collected all the food we possibly could and took it over to this Central Park Hooverville, where we got to know some of the men quite well.") In America as a whole were 12 million or so able-bodied unemployed, almost a fourth of the total national labor force. Marion, driving from the city toward Hyde Park just two or three days before, had picked up a teen-aged boy who was hitchhiking to Hudson, where, he had heard, there were jobs. "Last night when we sat down to supper my mother didn't sit down with us because there wasn't enough to go around," he said. "I'm the oldest, so it's up to me to get out." The response to all this by a Republican big-business administration seemed to Marion to be, for the most part, a helpless throwing up of hands. Sullen anger joined to a despair of democracy was rising ominously, to the Left and Right, out of the prevailing and spreading mass misery.

But Marion herself was in a buoyant mood as she left Hyde Park on a bright clear afternoon and headed northward in her Buick on Route 9. "It was a beautiful drive, always, along the Hudson, the Catskills all misty blue and green in the distance"—and also, for her as for everyone close to Franklin D. Roosevelt and personally involved in his destiny, the day was (as yesterday had been, as tomorrow would be) shot through with an electric excitement, a sense of active participation in history-making. This very journey was, to a slight degree, historical: she had been summoned to Albany to receive from FDR a confidential communication having to do with preparations for the forthcoming Democratic National Convention, to be delivered by her personally to two or three of his political lieutenants in upper New York.

She dined that evening, with the Governor and Missy, not in the mansion's great dining room but in the relatively cozy breakfast room. They sat at a small table having for its centerpiece a bowl of small, red early June roses. FDR was seemingly utterly relaxed, confident, cheerful, having received that day encouraging reports on his presidential nomination campaign from over the country. Missy was glowing. "It was a most happy meal."

At its end, the Governor asked Missy about her plans for the evening. She had work to do, said Missy ruefully. Whereupon he told Marion he had some after-dinner guests coming, "some pretty important ones," for an important conference; if she cared to "stay and listen" she was welcome to do so. He thought she might find it "interesting." She accepted his invitation, of course. (Later she wondered why he issued it. It was not out of a mere wish to amuse her, surely. Was it out of a desire to educate her toward a greater future usefulness to him? Was it out of a felt need for an appreciative witness to help him withstand, with the grace his circumstances required, pressures that he knew would be heavy and emotionally abrasive?)

Shortly thereafter three important Democratic leaders arrived and were ushered into a small downstairs study, where FDR awaited them in his wheelchair. Marion waited outside for a few minutes, as she had been asked to do, then slipped in and curled up "quiet as a mouse" on the davenport—FDR acknowledging her entrance with a smiling nod —where she listened, with increasing agitation, through four hours of talk.

The talk's subject was the hazard to FDR's presidential nomination posed by the Tammany mayor of New York City, playboy Jimmy Walker. Exposures of Tammany corruption had led to the Governor's appointment of Samuel Seabury, two years before, to investigate it in depth; Seabury's investigations had recently led him to make fifteen specific accusations of malfeasance and criminality on Walker's part, and Roosevelt was being sharply criticized for his failure thus far to take any action on the matter. The visitors in the study that night were certain that unless the Governor moved at once against the mayor, thereby proving his independence of Tammany and his commitment to public morality, he would lose the nomination; and they said so emphatically, even angrily, marshaling arguments that were convincing to Marion and clearly implied that Roosevelt was proving to be a temporizer, a weakling, a coward.

Throughout all this the Governor "remained remarkably calm," while steadfastly refusing to promise the action his visitors demanded. He bade them an unruffled, courteous goodnight when at last, confessing defeat, they left him, leaving behind the direst of threats and prophecies.

Marion, who was again to go to the convention as Caroline O'Day's alternate, was "shaken, deeply shaken." She sprang up as soon as she heard the front door close behind the visitors. "They're right, Franklin!" she cried. "You *know* they are! The Convention will never nominate a Tammany-controlled candidate, and that's what your enemies will call you. You *must* remove the mayor." He looked up at her. She was taken aback. "Seldom in the long years that I had known Franklin Roosevelt had I seen him really angry," she said later. His voice, though he still did not raise it, cut like a whip. "Never," he said, "*never* will I let it be said that I climbed to a position of power on the back of someone else!" Then, his long-pent exasperation having been vented on "one of the family," he took note of the fact that Marion "was really frightened" and went on to explain to her something of the dilemma he faced, and something—it was a rare revelation—of his basic decision-making processes.

He had hoped, naturally, that he could go into the Chicago convention with the solid support of the New York delegation. This proving impossible, he had hoped, naturally, to prevent the focusing upon him, at the convention, of Tammany's wrath. But as things now stood he certainly had less to fear from Tammany than from the alienation of support throughout the country that might ensue if he entered the convention with the Walker case unresolved. Hence there would be a net gain for him politically if he did as his visitors, and Marion, wanted him to do. But consider the moral implications: he was being asked to try and pass swift judgment upon a man from whose conviction he personally would profit, and every atom of his sense of fairness, of

100

justice, rebelled against his doing so. It was simply not "in character" for him to act as Marion, with the others, urged him to act, and he had found that to go against his own character was always a mistake in the long run.

Marion believes that her recollection of his following words is virtually verbatim:

"I have at times acted on the advice and counsel of others when it was contrary to my own judgment, and on occasion the results have been good. The advice proved to be good. But one act leads to another, and when the time comes to act again the same counselor may not be there. The first time, you acted out of character; the second time, you are confused. The path that you are following is not the one that you would have chosen by yourself, and because it isn't you make mistakes. This is a vital matter. It's more important than any immediate political advantage. You must let me be myself. Only when I am myself can I fit into my own pattern and find my way."

As things turned out, the Walker case was still pending when Marion and Nancy prepared to depart for Chicago, some three weeks later.

The Governor had by then sent the Seabury accusations to Walker, asking for a specific reply to each of them; Walker had announced he would not make such replies until after the convention, to which he was a delegate; and FDR was thereby condemned to run the last lap of his nomination race bearing the full weight of Tammany's wrath, along with a weight of doubt, of outright disapproval, on the part of many liberals and rural Americans. He could ill afford such extra burdens. He had more pledged delegate votes than all other contenders combined, but by the most optimistic estimate he was shy by some 80 votes of the two-thirds (770 votes) needed for the nomination. So what had seemed not long before to be the probability of a first-ballot nomination was reduced now to a mere possibility. And there loomed larger and larger another possibility, namely that FDR would fail of nomination on the first, second, or third ballots, whereupon his support would almost certainly crumble. A deadlocked convention would then, ultimately, nominate a compromise candidate.

Louis Howe, contemplating this possibility, grew almost frantic.

He wrote a one-and-a-half-minute "pep talk," which he had FDR record in warmly intimate tones, then sent one of the records along with an autographed photograph of FDR to every instructed Roosevelt delegate. ("That Louis!" says Marion, shaking her head in smiling remembrance.) He arranged to have an open-circuit telephone line between the Executive Mansion in Albany and the Roosevelt headquarters in the Congress Hotel in Chicago, with loudspeakers in the headquarters over which FDR could directly address individuals and delegations. To guard against information leaks, he sent out to run the headquarters switchboard Louise L. Hackmeister, the totally trustworthy and phenomenally skillful switchboard operator in the Albany mansion, who later ran the White House switchboard. He arranged for a direct private telephone line between the suite he himself was to occupy in the Congress Hotel, Room 1702 ("I'll never forget *that* number!" says Marion), and Roosevelt's study in the Executive Mansion. He tried to leave no detail to chance.

And as he labored his face became daily more drawn, his clothing more disheveled and streaked with cigarette ash, his disposition more irascible, his asthmatic breathing more difficult.

He came to Nancy and Marion on Thursday, June 23, just a few hours before they were to board the train for which they had made Pullman reservations.

"I want you to go out with me on the Twentieth Century Limited," he said flatly.

They protested. They would "love to," of course, but they were paying their own way. The Twentieth Century was an extra-fare train, and the expense was too great.

He merely gave them a look, a withering look, then stalked from the room.

Nancy turned to Marion.

"I guess we're taking the Twentieth Century," she said helplessly.

"I guess we are," Marion agreed.

They dined with Howe on the Limited that evening. They expected to breakfast with him next morning. He did not appear. Finally, very worried, they sent the conductor to his stateroom.

Howe lay there in his bed desperately ill, his face gray as he gasped for breath. "It was ghastly," says Marion. "Here he'd been living toward this moment since 1912!" They dared not so much as hint that he might have to enter a hospital in Chicago.

By the time the train pulled in at the station, however, he had managed by sheer willpower to overcome his asthma sufficiently to dress and take a cab, with the two women, to the hotel. There he at once took command of a sadly deteriorating situation. Already, before the convention had formally opened, the talk was loud that Roosevelt "has been stopped"; that Al Smith, who had come to Chicago bitterly determined to win the nomination for himself, could never make it; that therefore Newton D. Baker, who had been Woodrow Wilson's Secretary of War, would be the nominee, though there was also some slight chance that the choice would be Speaker of the House John Nance Garner of Texas, whom the reactionary press lord William Randolph Hearst was backing.

For feverish days and nights thereafter, Louis Howe lay in Room 1702, stretched out on bed or sofa or floor struggling for breath, his drawn gray face blasted by electric fans. And because he lay there—his brain afire, his fierce spirit raging against the frailties of his pain-racked body, his hand never more than a few inches from his direct wire to FDR—Room 1702 became a vital center of the whole vast, confused nominating process in Chicago. Into that room poured information from every quarter of the convention. Out of it radiated terse messages from Albany and crackling orders to Roosevelt workers in the hotel corridors, in the campaign headquarters, at the stadium.

Roosevelt was put into nomination on the afternoon of June 20 by the man who had launched him in politics in 1910, Judge Mack of Poughkeepsie. The band burst into "Anchors Aweigh," and played it over and over again while FDR's supporters demonstrated—until

Howe, listening to the radio, felt he simply couldn't bear any more of it. "For God's sake tell them to play something else—anything else!" he rasped into the phone, whereupon the band began to play "Happy Days Are Here Again," the song ever afterward associated with FDR.

When the convention had adjourned until eight in the evening, on the day of the nominating speeches, Marion and Nancy came to Louis's room and did what little they could to help him. They answered the door, tidied up a little, ran errands. Jim Farley dropped by for a little while. He and Howe talked while sitting together on the floor, eating chocolate ice cream that Marion had ordered. "Louis drank very little, and Farley didn't drink at all," she explains, "and they wanted refreshment." Then Farley left. Nancy and Marion remained with Louis as the convention again went into session and the speeches continued, droning out of the radio loudspeaker, its volume turned low, while Howe received and made one phone call after another.

"He looked like death," says Marion. "It was just terribly hot in Chicago, and in those days, you know, nothing was air-conditioned excepting movie theaters and drugstores. Jim told me he wondered if Louis could live through the convention, and I wondered, too. The only part of him that seemed absolutely alive were his eyes. They seemed to blaze out of their sockets. He was in his shirtsleeves, of course, with the collar open, and that scrawny neck seemed scrawnier than ever. His shirt was soaked with sweat. It clung to his thin arms and bony chest. Every now and then he doubled over, coughing in the most horrible way, though that didn't keep him from smoking one cigarette after another." Hours passed before she and Nan went back to the stadium. "When I left Louis, he was lying on top of the bureau," Marion remembers. "He thought he got more air up there."

The rest of that long night and all the crucial day that followed was, in Marion's direct experience of it, a blurred confusion of dire forebodings and suspenseful excitement. She remembers going to a window of the stadium during the brief pause between the last seconding speech and the first ballot and noting, with surprise, that the buildings across the way were silhouetted against a faintly dawn-washed sky: it was

4:30 in the morning of Friday, July 1. She remembers the three ballots that followed as a long-drawn-out mingling of suspense and exasperation and boredom, crowned with fearful disappointment. When, at 9:15, the exhausted convention at last adjourned until evening, the longed-for stampede to Roosevelt seemed farther away than it had when the balloting began. On the third ballot he had 683 votes. This was 492¾ more than Al Smith, his closest rival, and 581¾ more than Garner, in third place, but it was 87 votes less than the needed two-thirds. Marion can never forget how depressed they all were. Jim Farley had said the Roosevelt lines were not likely to hold beyond the fourth ballot.

In the mad rush for taxis, Marion was separated from her friends. When she finally found a cab and climbed wearily in, a man climbed in simultaneously on the other side. There ensued a brief conflict of wills ("I wasn't giving it up, he wasn't giving it up"), amicably ending when they discovered they were both going to the Congress Hotel and were both for Roosevelt. Worn, disheveled, frankly anxious about their candidate's chances, they breakfasted together in the Congress coffee shop—"and that," says Marion, "was the beginning of my friendship with Sumner Welles." Then, with Nancy, Marion mounted to Room 1702, where they found Louis Howe lying on a mattress in the center of the floor, in the windblast of two electric fans. And for all the rest of the fervid day they did Howe's bidding and shared all his swift fluctuations of mood.

When Jim Farley came into 1702, sometime before noon, and lay down on the mattress beside Louis to whisper into his ear, the mood was darkly pessimistic. Mississippi was reported to have switched from Roosevelt to Garner. Other southern states were sure to follow suit. The possibility of a Smith-Garner coalition, nonexistent yesterday, now seemed real—and if Garner refused this, as still seemed likely, the long balloting that followed must lead ultimately to Baker, or Governor Ritchie of Maryland, or some as yet unnamed dark horse. "Texas is our only hope!" That is what Farley whispered into Howe's ear, as Marion, who was a witness to this famous interchange, was told at once. Howe agreed. Farley departed to hold conference with Sam Rayburn, head of the Texas delegation.

Then it was that FDR received his reward for what had seemed to his wife, and virtually all liberals, a disgraceful retreat from principle, five months before.

In response to virulent attacks upon his "internationalism" by isolationist Hearst, who had declared for Garner because Garner stood for "America first," Roosevelt on February 2 had publicly repudiated his former support of American membership in the League of Nations. Marion remembers how furious Eleanor had been about this—how she would not so much as speak to her husband for days thereafter—and Marion herself had been, with Nancy, gravely "disappointed."

But now it came clear—*seemingly* clear, at any rate—that FDR's humiliating capitulation to a man he knew to be contemptible, and his tacit avowal of an isolationism he knew to be mistaken were the price he had had to pay if he were to become President of the United States. By noon of July 1 Hearst realized that Garner's continuance in the race would probably lead to the nomination of either Smith or Baker, the former of whom had long been his bitter enemy, the latter of whom he detested for "visionary Wilsonianism." Hearst therefore urged Garner to withdraw and "throw his delegates to Governor Roosevelt." Garner did as Hearst advised, out of his determination to avoid a deadlocked convention. And as Texas went, so went California—with other states sure to break to Roosevelt thereafter. By 6:30 or so, his nomination was assured, with the subsequent nomination of Garner for the Vice-Presidency also being assured, this being necessary to swing the Texas delegation to FDR.

"We knew we had it when we went back to the stadium," says Marion, "but it was a beautifully kept secret. When I went by Governor Smith's box I stopped to say hello to him and Mrs. Smith, as I always did, and he said, 'Ah, tonight's the night.' He was sure Franklin was stopped, that the convention would stampede to him. I said, 'Well, Governor, let's say, let the best man win.' "

Then the fourth ballot began. When the chairman called for California, McAdoo strode to the platform and the hall was suddenly hushed. California, said McAdoo, "did not come here to deadlock this convention. . . ." He looked up at the galleries packed by Mayor Cermack of Chicago with noisy Smith men. ". . . When any man comes into a Democratic National Convention with the popular will behind him to the extent of almost seven hundred votes . . ." He was interrupted by a roar from the floor, a roar of angry disapproval from the galleries, and could not go on until the Smith claque was quieted. "California," concluded McAdoo, "casts forty-four votes for Franklin D. Roosevelt!"

"And then the stampede began," Marion remembers. "But our New York delegation remained split, and the nomination was never made unanimous."

Most of what Marion thereafter witnessed in Chicago is history long known to all: the announcement that FDR would fly to Chicago to make—unprecedentedly—his acceptance speech; Al Smith's angry refusal to remain in Chicago to greet the nominee ("—oh, he was bitter, so terribly bitter, and shortly after that I went to a luncheon in New York City and was placed next to Mrs. Smith, and she asked to be moved"); Howe's emergence from the Congress Hotel to meet FDR's plane and ride with the nominee in an open car through the streets, pressing upon the nominee as he did so the draft speech he had stayed up all night to write, since the one that had been read to him from Albany was, in his judgment, "awful"; FDR's reading of the opening page of the Howe draft at the convention, and then proceeding with the Albany draft ("I pledge you," said FDR, "I pledge myself, to a new deal for the American people").

But Marion was involved in one historically interesting episode of which nothing was published for nearly forty years. On June 30, the day of the nominating speeches, Nan had received from Eleanor Roosevelt a letter in which Eleanor poured out in tumbled, passionate phrases her woe at the prospect of becoming First Lady of the United States. She couldn't bear it, she said; she just "could not live in the White House." On the night of July 1, when Marion and Nancy returned to Howe's room they found him on his feet, reanimated by the triumph, glowing with it, but still tensely anxious that something might yet go terribly wrong. The two women were more afraid than he because of Eleanor's letter. Nancy had it with her. She handed it to Howe. His pale face darkened as he read it, his lips drew into a thin line, and when he had finished he ripped the letter into shreds, tiny shreds, and dropped these into a wastebasket.

"You are not to breathe a word of this to anyone, understand?" he ordered sternly. "Not to *anyone* . . ."

N I N E

WHAT Eleanor Roosevelt faced, and feared more than ever before, on the eve of her husband's nomination for the Presidency, a nomination that appeared tantamount to his election, was the imminent extinction of the independent life she had made for herself. The White House had to be for her a much more exacting post than the Executive Mansion had been, and there seemed to her little chance of her doing as First Lady in Washington what she had managed to do as First Lady in Albany. A measure of her desperate unhappiness is the confession in her memoirs that, after his election, she "tentatively suggested to my husband that perhaps merely being hostess at the necessary formal functions would not take all my time and he might like me to do a real job and take over some of his mail. He merely looked at me quizzically and said he did not think that would do, that Missy, who had been handling his mail for a long time, would feel I was interfering. I knew he was right . . . but it was a last effort to keep in close touch and to feel that I had a real job to do."

But of course it was *not* a last effort—and in the end, as we know, for it is history, Eleanor Roosevelt fashioned a public life that derived much sustenance from her husband's fame, from his vast store of official power, yet was uniquely her own; and from it a very considerable feedback was poured into that fame and power out of which it partially came. From her first day in the White House she played gracefully the role of symbolic person imposed upon her as the President's wife, but she quickly managed to make this a relatively minor one of her activities. Within a few months she was more firmly established in the national public mind than she had ever been in the mind of her native state as a sharply defined personality, a forceful mind, an acutely sensitive conscience, a remarkably strong moral character.

And for this fortunate development Louis Howe deserved, and received from Eleanor, much credit. He had ridiculed her terrors during the months preceding her husband's nomination—had spoken to her in verse of the "hooded brotherhood of fears" that "all these futile years" had "filled your timid soul with numbing dread" when all she had to do ("fool" he called her) was face this "brotherhood" and tear the "masking cowls aside." As for her having "nothing important to do" once she was in the White House, this was utter nonsense: she would have far more and greater opportunities to "do good" than ever before. And between the election and the inauguration he helped her to locate and plan her attack upon these opportunities.

He had, nevertheless, a profoundly empathic understanding of her anxieties, for he had similar anxieties of his own as election day came and passed—a bitter fear that he would be shunted aside. He wanted desperately to be chief secretary to the President. He could not but feel that he deserved the post. But there were dark hours during which he was convinced that FDR must decide, however regretfully, that this post was too prominent for so ugly, sickly, and irascible an old man.

A scowling gloom had settled upon him on election day evening, though the first returns presaged a landslide FDR victory. He had

110

refused to remain in the suite in New York City's Biltmore Hotel where Roosevelt and a few intimates were listening to the returns. Instead he had gone across the street to his campaign office and there, secluded with his wife and son, had remained until Eleanor and Jim Farley came for him, on FDR's orders, and escorted him back to the hotel, it being by then clear that FDR would carry forty-two states. In the hotel suite he had been greeted before newsmen by FDR as one of "the two people in the United States" (Farley was the other) who "more than anybody else" was "responsible for this great victory"; but this had not allayed his fear. He continued apprehensive that the chief secretaryship would go to either Marvin McIntyre or Steve Early, each of whom was a former reporter who had served FDR during the 1920 vice-presidential campaign (hence an original member of the Cuff Links Club), each of whom had rendered yeoman's service during the campaign just ended, and each of whom was far more personable than Louis Howe.

Marion vividly recalls the night in late January of 1933 when the decision on this matter was made known by FDR. It was at the annual Cuff Links dinner, held that year in the cottage at Val Kill some days prior to FDR's actual birthday, since he was to be in Warm Springs on January 30. "The occasion was hilarious, as always," says Marion. "Louis had arranged a most amazing and amusing menu, and had written one of his funniest skits. I had to wear my riding clothes, I remember, because I had the part of a Western Union messenger bringing telegrams to the President-elect from important people all over the world. The messages Louis had concocted were simply killing." All the same, there was a tension between Howe, McIntyre, and Early that all of them felt until, at precisely the right moment, FDR announced that Louis would be his chief secretary, that McIntyre would be appointments secretary and Early press secretary, "and everyone relaxed, happily," Marion goes on. "For we all felt this was the right choice for Franklin to make. Even McIntyre and Early thought so, I'm sure."

(A year later, Steve Early as presidential press secretary had some anxiety about the Cuff Links Club celebration prepared by Howe and held in the upstairs hall of the White House. Opponents of the New Deal were by then charging that FDR aspired to play in the history of the American Republic a role analogous to those played by Julius Caesar and Augustus in the final years of the Roman Republic—that is, he aspired to be dictator and/or emperor—and Howe's skit dealt comically with this theme. ["Dear Caesar" was the salutation generally employed by Adolph A. Berle of the celebrated Brain Trust in personal letters to FDR during this period.] FDR, clad in purple toga, crowned with laurel, played emperor with gusto, striking imperious poses and mugging delightedly. An armor-clad, spear-bearing Louis Howe was an unlikely member of the Praetorian Guard. "Eleanor represented the Delphic Oracle—it was a crazy mixed-up kind of skit, you see—and issued strange prophecies regarding the New Deal." A photograph taken of this gala affair is published in this book for the first time, Marion having at last decided that the stern letter with which Steve Early accompanied the pictures when they were sent out to the birthday celebrants is no longer "operative," as a later White House press secretary would have put it. Wrote Early in February of 1934: "The photographs made at the birthday dinner this year are given to each member of the gang with the understanding that each of the pictures shall be safeguarded against duplication. . . . It is respectfully requested that none of these photographs be exhibited or that their existence be discovered by any outsider. These photographs belong to the gang and to the gang alone. Should they escape from your care and keeping, dire punishment will be imposed. Be warned, be careful, or be banished to the regions where the faithless, false, fraudulent, deceitful, unscrupulous, and perfidious felons abide.")

Thus Howe, moving into the White House with the Roosevelts, was enabled to continue to serve, as he had done for a dozen years, as a bridge linking FDR's and Eleanor's activities, or as a vital cement that "held things together" (so Marion puts it) within the intimate Roosevelt circle. He who had helped Eleanor to launch the Women's Democratic publication after she was in the White House ("The 'News' is very shy of 'news' this month & we haven't made it up yet!" ran a typical note on White House stationery to Nancy Cook) was delighted with the chatty, personal-letter type of column entitled "Passing Thoughts of Mrs. Franklin D. Roosevelt" that she wrote for each issue from February 1933 until the *News* ceased publication at the end of 1935. When it was suggested that she hold regular press conferences, an unprecedented thing for a First Lady to do, he heartily approved (so did FDR), and she happily followed the suggestion.

Howe acted as Eleanor's literary agent in 1933 and 1934, negotiating for her a contract with the North American Newspaper Alliance, whereby she received $500 apiece for monthly 750-word articles, and a contract with the magazine *Woman's Home Companion*, whereby she received $1,000 apiece for monthly letter-answering columns headed "I Want You to Write to Me." (He subsequently placed her with a professional literary agent, George Bye, who later negotiated the sale of first serial and book publication rights of *This Is My Story* to the *Ladies Home Journal* and to Harper and Brothers.) And it was with Louis Howe's very forceful encouragement that she became a professional lecturer, touring—necessarily in brief stints—under the management of one of the nation's top lecture circuit impresarios. ("The trip has gone fairly well," she wrote Nancy from Dayton, Ohio, while on her first lecture tour in March of 1936, "but they want you to work all day as the wife of the Pres. & then be a good lecturer at night & travel on after that is over to the next place! However, I suppose $3,000 check is worth one week of it.") By then she had become a syndicated newspaper columnist whose 400- to 500-word "My Day"— dictated to Tommy (Malvina Thompson, her secretary) on trains and planes, in hotel rooms and automobiles, in snatched moments in the White House, at Val Kill during a picnic, even from a sickbed while running a high fever—was daily distributed by United Features to some five dozen newspapers with a combined circulation of more than 4 million. (Being now financially independent, she gave much of what she earned to organizations and causes to which she was committed.)

And Howe not only helped to bridge FDR's and Eleanor's public activities, he also helped to involve her most intimate friends in New Deal programs, enabling her to continue the weaving together of her private and public lives, and selves, into a single if quite widely various pattern. Integral to that pattern were Val-Kill Industries and the Todhunter School. For she clung more closely than ever to Marion and Nancy—she seemed to need their friendship more than ever—during the years immediately following her husband's presidential election. She continued her teaching schedule at Todhunter through the first semester of the 1932–1933 school year and invited to the inaugural on Saturday, March 4, 1933, all the girls of the school, with their parents.

She had Marion and Nancy close by her through all that cloudy, chilly day. They attended the morning prayer service conducted for Roosevelt in St. John's Episcopal Church by his old teacher, the Reverend Endicott Peabody, rector of Groton School, who had married Eleanor to Franklin in 1905. They were present at the Capitol when Roosevelt took the oath of office and delivered to a fearful, depression-ridden nation his heartening inaugural address (". . . the only thing we have to fear is fear itself. . . . This nation asks for action. . . . We must act, and act quickly. . . ."). They were at the huge afternoon reception in the White House, and at the ball that night, and they slept that night in the White House.

Marion had to return to New York City next day to be at Todhunter, but Nancy stayed on in the White House for eight days or so "to help Eleanor make the second floor into a living quarters for the Roosevelt family," as Marion says. "They found that the brass bed in Franklin's room was too short, so Nan made, in the shop, a fine four-poster bed of extra length when she got back to the cottage. The President used it for as long as he was in the White House. Nancy also made a four-poster for Eleanor's use in the White House."

As soon as school was out, Marion, with Nancy, returned to the White House for several days, during which the three friends made

114

plans relating to FDR's first presidential vacation—this to be taken when Congress adjourned.

Certainly he had earned a vacation by the end of what has become known in history as "the hundred days of the first New Deal." By June 17 the national economy, which had ground to an almost total halt with the collapse of the nation's credit structure on March 4, was moving again, slowly reviving with the aid of strong and various actions—unprecedented in peacetime—by the federal government. The banks, closed in a national bank holiday ordered the day after the inauguration, had been reopened with federal safeguards for deposits. The gold standard had been abandoned in favor of a managed currency. An act establishing a Civilian Conservation Corps; a Federal Emergency Relief Act, providing for direct federal relief for individuals in economic distress; acts establishing the Tennessee Valley Authority (TVA); the Agricultural Adjustment Administration (AAA); the National Recovery Administration (NRA)—all these had been pushed through Congress in less time than any one of them would normally have required.

And now came one of the memorable episodes of Marion's Roosevelt years. FDR decided that his vacation would be a cruise, with James, John, and Franklin, Jr., northeastward along the New England coast aboard the schooner *Amberjack II*, ending at Campobello, which he had not seen since he was carried from it, polio-paralyzed, in 1921. While he sailed, Eleanor, Nancy, and Marion were to drive up from Hyde Park and prepare the Campobello cottage for his coming. They did so, stopping for the night of June 25 with their friend, Mary Dreier, a leading social reformer, at her home in Southwest Harbor on Mount Desert Island—and next morning they awoke to find the *Amberjack II* anchored offshore. "We were excited. We'd had no idea where they were. . . ." The three Roosevelt sons came ashore to breakfast with their mother and her friends. "Then the President asked us to join him on the *Amberjack*. We did, and the newspapers took pictures of us that were published widely. I had clippings sent me from England and Denmark." Before noon the *Amberjack* had sailed; and shortly thereafter Eleanor, Marion, and Nancy drove on to Lubec, Maine, whence they rode the car ferry to Campobello.

"We opened the house. The island at that time was rather a primitive place; and getting ready for the big picnic we were to have when the President arrived took all of Nancy's expertise, along with a lot of neighborliness on the part of the island women. We had some of them bake rolls, others cook a huge ham, others prepare great bowls of potato salad, and so on—because there was to be at this picnic a large number of people, including the Governor of Maine, Norman H. Davis, Henry Morgenthau, Canadian officials, dozens of Navy officers, and many local Roosevelt friends. Louis Howe was there, of course."

Came the morning of Thursday, June 29. A dismal morning. As the scheduled hour for the President's arrival approached there was fog so thick that it blotted from the sight of those ashore the cruiser U.S.S. *Indianapolis*, the Coast Guard cutter *Cuyahoga*, other various small craft, and the local herring fleet ("properly dressed for the occasion"), all anchored off Welchpool. Anxiety was as thick as the fog. Could the *Amberjack* safely navigate the dangerous Lubec Narrows? Then, as so often happened for FDR on public occasions, the weather broke in his favor: at precisely the hour when he was supposed to arrive the fog lifted, as if some giant, invisible hand had raised a curtain. The sun shone brightly out of a cloudless sky "and the schooner sailed quite majestically through the Narrows and tacked across Passamaquoddy Bay, and Franklin landed at Welchpool for the first time in a dozen years."

Some days later Marion sailed from New York City for a vacation in England. On her return she conveyed to FDR orally a message given her in strictest confidence, for the President's ears only, by her friend, Lady Nancy Astor, whose house guest she had been for a weekend at Cliveden. Lady Astor, born a Langhorne of Virginia, was a cousin of William C. Bullitt of Philadelphia, who had recently become an FDR confidant; and her message to the President was a warning against

Bullitt. "I've known Billy well since he was a child," said Nancy Langhorne Astor, "and I *know* that he is absolutely untrustworthy. The President will be making a great mistake if he places Bill in a position of great trust and responsibility." FDR, who had been a friend of the Waldorf Astors for decades,* received Marion's message without comment.

---

* In the letter-diary he wrote during his European mission in the summer of 1918, Roosevelt told of finding "Mrs. Astor [Waldorf Astor was not yet a Lord in that year] . . . the same enthusiastic, amusing, and talkative soul as always. . . ."

T E N

W H I L E Marion was abroad in mid-August of 1933, Eleanor Roosevelt, at the behest of Clarence Pickett, the Quaker social activist who was executive secretary of the American Friends Service Committee, made a memorable anonymous automobile trip into the mining country of West Virginia whose scenes Marion had been appalled by a decade before. Conditions there were worse now than they had been then. Mines had been shut down for years, or were operating only at far-spaced intervals. Thousands of men, many permanently blacklisted because they had dared to strike—and had lost—in the past, lived with their gaunt wives and hollow-eyed, belly-bloated children in literally nauseating squalor, huddled in miserable hovels whose inadequate water supply was drawn in some cases from the polluted stream that served them as sewer. As shocking to Eleanor as the physical misery of these people was their utter hopelessness—the dull, listless despair that caused them to sit on their sagging porch steps hour after hour staring blankly into space. She returned from her trip convinced that nowhere in all the land could there be more imperative need for the government in Washington to "act, and act quickly" (as her husband had promised in his inaugural address), than in the rural slums of West Virginia.

It had been at the President's personal request that Congress had appropriated $25 million for expenditure in 1933 to facilitate establishment of what he called "subsistence homesteads," meaning small farms where families could raise their own food, with some surplus for sale, while earning cash income from part-time employment in local industries. The idea was part and parcel of his and Eleanor's long-held conviction—a conviction that had initially animated Val-Kill Industries—that the concentration of the national population in huge cities would be a disaster for America, that the Republic's good health in the twentieth century required an approximately fifty-fifty mixture of city and country, industry and agriculture. The appropriation had gone to the Public Works Administration, headed by Secretary of the Interior Harold Ickes. Ickes had at once established a Subsistence Homestead Division of PWA, and at the President's specific suggestion, had appointed as its chief M. L. Wilson, a former professor of agriculture economics at Montana State College, a leading philosopher of farming as a way of life and a warm, lovable personality.

It was to Wilson that Ickes directed Eleanor when she, with Clarence Pickett, turned to him for help. The farm philosopher, First Lady, and Pickett established an immediate rapport. More important was Louis Howe's intense interest in what Eleanor proposed—an interest stemming in part, one suspects, from his concern with Roosevelt family relations, but also from his own conviction that urban congestion was an evil that subsistence homesteads, in conjunction with industrial decentralization, might cure or prevent. Eleanor called at once upon Nancy Cook, the Val-Kill Industries manager, for advice and counsel regarding the establishment of handicraft industry in the distressed region.

119

Soon—with a precipitous rapidity, as a matter of fact, because of spur and whip applied from the President's office by Louis Howe—the Subsistence Homestead Division had acquired by purchase a 1,200-acre tract, known as the Arthur Farm, near the little town of Reedsville, some fifteen miles southeast of Morgantown, West Virginia; and there Wilson and a local staff, under what amounted to direct administrative supervision by Louis Howe and Eleanor, were engaged in establishing the first Subsistence Homestead Project, called Arthurdale. Here would rise—this was the dream—an economically self-sufficient community inhabited by ex-miners and their families who made their livings partly from the land, partly from local factory employment, while engaging in arts and crafts; various cultural activities, including music, drama, folk dancing; and a progressive educational program for adults as well as children. To head the local school, which was to be the center of community life, Eleanor was to employ one of John Dewey's disciples, Elsie Clapp.

When Marion returned from Europe in the first week of September, her two closest friends were already deeply immersed in this pioneering enterprise, which at once became an important part of her life also, though she could take no active part in it because of her commitment to Todhunter.

It was not, however, a wholly happy experience. In part this was due to the irritable impatience of Louis Howe. As Secretary Ickes noted in his diary on December 2, 1933, Howe "in a rash moment told the President that we could start work [at Reedsville] within three weeks" after the land purchase was made. "The result has been, in order to make good on this rash boast, that we have rushed ahead pell-mell. I am afraid that we are spending more money than we have a right to spend." Howe's greatest blunder was to order by phone, for $1,000 apiece, fifty prefabricated houses designed for summer occupancy on Cape Cod. They were not only too flimsy for winter shelter, they were also too small for the concrete foundations that had already been poured when, knocked down, they arrived at Reedsville. Hence it was impossible for the three dozen families who had by then been moved into the Arthur house, or into tents on its grounds, to assemble the prefabs for occupancy before winter, as originally planned. Architect Eric Gugler was then called by Eleanor to redesign the houses (wrote Eleanor to M. L. Wilson on November 17, 1933: ". . . I have taken on Nancy Cook and Eric Gugler as advisory experts on the housing end," adding that they were to be paid expenses plus a fee "not in excess of $30 a day, which I understand is the standard pay for experts"); and Gugler, approaching the problem from a strictly architectural point of view, had solved it by adding to the prefabs "wings, bay windows, fire places, porches, terraces, and pergolas," as a hostile critic wrote in an August 1934 issue of the *Saturday Evening Post.* Costs soared to some $10,000 per family, which was three or four times the amount at first projected.

"I don't see how we can possibly defend ourselves on this project," confided Ickes to his diary on March 10, 1934. "It worries me more than anything else in my whole Department." Two weeks later he called Wilson, Pickett, and Gugler into his office, where he "expressed" himself "in no uncertain terms about the way this project has been managed." Gugler angrily defended himself, saying "that more money had been spent than he had been in favor of spending but that the committee [supervising Arthurdale] had insisted on his doing what he had done." By "the committee" Gugler meant Eleanor Roosevelt, Ickes was sure. Gugler also pointed out that the fifty houses Howe had brought "were a joke" and that he had had "to go to great trouble and expense to make them habitable." A few hours later Ickes was summoned to Howe's office, where Howe told him that "Mrs. Roosevelt was hitting the ceiling about my criticism of Reedsville," which she was interpreting, with justification—though Ickes denied it—as a criticism of her own ability. Back in his own office, Ickes "found out from a call by Wilson that he and his two colleagues went back to Wilson's office where they sat down with Miss Cook, Mrs. Roosevelt's friend . . . and reiterated to her my general criticisms. Miss Cook went over to Mrs. Roosevelt so that she must have gotten a highly distorted report." Rueful was Ickes's conclusion to his diary entry for that March 20: "All in all it has not been what I would call a successful day."

Nor was Louis's house-buying error the only major error that caused Arthurdale to be, in the end, "a dream that failed," as Marion puts it. The very location of the project proved to be an error. Because of Howe's and Eleanor's haste, adequate tests were not made of the Arthur tract before it was purchased, and its soil turned out to be ill suited to commercial crops, while its substratum of porous rock "caused great expense in making the water supply safe." When finally completed in the summer of 1934, the Arthurdale settlement "was assuredly attractive, and the whole project did make the people of this area, who had suffered for years under the neglect of absentee landlordism, believe that the government cared." There was also, for a time, an unusually rich community life, with Elsie Clapp, Nancy, and Eleanor at the heart of it. ("Eleanor asked Nan to come to Arthurdale to direct and help the men to make furniture for their houses while their wives were weaving rugs," says Marion. "Nan headed the handicraft center there. She was eager to do it, though it meant frequent long journeys from New York and new responsibilities added to her already heavy schedule with the State Democratic Committee and Val-Kill Industries. I think the tremendous strain of those years undermined her health and shortened her life. She grew so tired!")

But hard efforts on Eleanor's part failed to attract to the area enough industry to employ more than a third of the available labor at any time, and the project became the target of vicious and unremitting political attack. Private contributions, which had subsidized Elsie Clapp's school and other elements of Arthurdale's community life, declined. Ultimately, the school, in which Eleanor had taken particular pride, encountered opposition from the very people it served. "I'm afraid it was a bit too progressive for the homesteaders," Marion explains. "They began to feel that their children were not being taught the fundamentals—the three Rs—as they should be. So Elsie, with her teaching staff, had to move out—to another community. The Arthur-

122

dale school then became part of West Virginia's public education system."

Of Marion's personal memories of Arthurdale, some of the most vivid are from a vacation automobile trip that she, Eleanor, and Nancy took in late June and early July 1934. From Arthurdale they drove to Asheville, North Carolina, then to Norris, Tennessee, where they toured TVA projects under the guidance of Arthur E. Morgan, chairman of the three-man TVA board of directors; then on to Berea College in Kentucky, the University of Kentucky, and the Century of Progress Exposition (World's Fair) in Chicago, where Eleanor's two days "were made most uncomfortable" because "she was pursued by photographers and crowds wherever she went. We would get up early and slip through one of the least-frequented gates, paying our way, hoping to be accepted as ordinary tourists, but always she was recognized almost at once." Eleanor had trouble, too, with reporters and photographers when she flew west from Chicago to be with her daughter Anna, who was in Reno divorcing Curtis Dall.

Yet while Eleanor thus mingled her private and public lives during these years, exposing her intimate friends every now and then to the glare of publicity in which she perforce had to live, she also managed to maintain, with these friends, a strictly private life—and in this Earl Miller continued to play an important part. In May of 1932 he became engaged to Ruth Bellinger, and Eleanor insisted upon having the wedding at Hyde Park a few weeks later. Anna Roosevelt Dall was bridesmaid; Elliott was best man; and Ruth and Earl spent their wedding night in Val Kill Cottage. In the late summer of 1933 Earl and Ruth (and in 1934 Earl alone) joined Eleanor and Nancy for vacations in a hideaway resort on Chazy Lake in upper New York—fun-filled carefree holidays much photographed by Nancy's and Earl's still and movie cameras. One movie sequence was the acting out of a scenario concocted by Nancy and Earl, with suggestions from the others. It was entitled "The Kidnapping of the First Lady," and in it Earl played a double role. Dressed as a pirate, he sneaked up behind Eleanor as she sat knitting on the resort cottage terrace and carried her off, depositing her in a rowboat, rowing her across the water, and tying her to a tree. Her place was taken on the terrace by Nancy, who picked up the dropped knitting needles, and plied them in mugging imitation of Eleanor. Later, Eleanor was rescued, and all ended happily.

Less happy by far was the ending, a few months later, of Earl's second marriage. Eleanor spoke of it in an undated letter from the White House to "Nan darling," asking her to "order the mattress & springs & 2 pillows" for rooms Earl had taken in Glens Falls (he was now chief inspector of prison guards in New York). Eleanor went on, "He wants to hurry his own rooms & he wants the simplest possible bookcase to go with his furniture . . . & has his desk a chair? I'll give him these things for Xmas & birthday so send the bill to me!"

Earl continued to be often at Val Kill Cottage, and was frequent overnight guest in the small and virtually secret apartment Eleanor shared with Tommy in Greenwich Village as a means of privacy when she came to New York City (he often used it when Eleanor was in Washington). ". . . Earl was in N.Y. Sat. & is at the apartment till Friday morning of this week working," ran a letter from the White House to Nancy, "but he caught a bad cold again & hoped he could work there & not go up town any more than was necessary. He would like to come down Feb. 13th & bring his latest girl & her mother for lunch and send them back by train & stay himself till he goes to Val Kill for the next week. Will this be convenient for all of you? I will stay & come to N.Y. on Monday morning with you." (She added that she would "be with you again at the cottage . . . for the night" of February 22 "but F. gets there Tuesday so I will have to go to the big house after breakfast!")

E L E V E N

A NECDOTAL, with the anecdotes revelatory of various facets of a bewilderingly multifaceted personality, are Marion's personal remembrances of Franklin Delano Roosevelt as President of the United States.

Thus:

Among the men for whom FDR had little use in the spring of 1933, judging from derogatory remarks which Marion heard him make in the bosom of the family, was Norman H. Davis. The handsome, white-haired, wealthy Davis, who had operated since Wilson days as ambassador at large of the American Executive, was of the conservative wing of the Democratic party; he was inclined toward Herbert Hoover's view that the American Depression was caused by events abroad and could be cured only in concert with European nations, a view FDR flatly repudiated; and his approach to monetary policy was generally that of international bankers, whose mentality and morality were, in FDR's expressed views, contemptible. Yet Marion observed that in late June of 1933, when FDR and Davis were working on Campobello, FDR treated Davis as an "old crony" for whom he had great admiration and affection. This struck Marion as hypocritical, and she said so bluntly when she and FDR were alone together. The charge evidently disturbed him. He denied it, saying that while he strongly disagreed with Davis on some matters, and even morally disapproved of him in some ways,* there were other matters on which he and Davis agreed and other aspects of Davis of which he thoroughly approved. "Don't you realize that you seldom find a person who agrees with you in everything and pleases you in every way?" he went on. "It's ridiculous to expect it. When you find a person who cares deeply for something for which you care deeply, you work with him on that, and you don't drag in other things which would cause differences." This was "very characteristic of him," says Marion. "It was why some people thought him lacking in frankness."

And indeed, without necessarily clearing him of the charge of "two-facedness," his defense of his conduct with regard to Davis does suggest a general truth whose recognition by him was important to his career. Every human being is unique, and none is perfectly self-consistent in terms of abstract, mutually exclusive categories labeled "kind" or "cruel," "loving" or "hateful," "selfish" or "generous," and so on. Instead each is a mixture of the oppositional traits so categorized. Yet between almost any two human beings, and certainly among any thousand, are common denominators—a common humanity—that make human community not only possible but necessary for individual happiness and full self-realization. It is with and of these commonalities, while also maintaining respect for individuality and diversity, that a successful democratic politics is made. "You don't have to be

---

* Davis's was one of the names appearing on a then recently exposed (by a Senate investigating committee) "preferred list" of those to whom the House of Morgan had, on occasion in the 1920s, secretly offered stock at prices below the current market.

100 percent with a person," is the way Marion puts it. "You've got to pick out the things that are vital to you—and if, on the big issues, you are in agreement, all right. That was one of the things he definitely taught me."

From this it followed that one could sincerely be a friend of another without taking on that other's personal enmities as one's own. Thus Marion remained sincerely and warmly a friend of both Under Secretary of State Sumner Welles and Secretary Hull, though the Secretary soon cordially disliked the Under Secretary and came ultimately to hate him, finally forcing Welles's resignation, with FDR's reluctant acquiescence. "Because I was devoted to both of them, I felt terrible about the rift," says Marion, "but I could see so easily how it happened." In the summer of 1935 she lived for several weeks in the White House while working as an assistant to Aubrey Williams on the launching of the National Youth Administration (NYA), in which Eleanor took special interest. Since the NYA office was nearby, Marion generally lunched in the White House—and often, leaving after lunch, she would meet Sumner Welles coming in, "just dropping by to see the President for a few minutes, as it was perfectly natural for him to do because they came from the same social background, had both gone to Groton and Harvard, and had known each other since Welles was a child." Hull didn't have this kind of relationship with the President; naturally he feared and resented a subordinate who was closer to the center of power than he—and FDR, it must be said, did little to alleviate Hull's anxieties in this regard.

His wish to alleviate them, however, may have prompted the response he made to Marion's questions about U.S. policy toward the Spanish civil war, which broke out in July of 1936. Marion was, from the outset, strongly pro-Loyalist. So, she believed, was the President. Yet the President, invoking a recently passed Neutrality Act (though he might have avoided doing so on the plausible ground that the act failed to apply to civil wars), embargoed the shipment of desperately needed arms to Spanish Loyalists while Hitler and Mussolini were sending munitions, planes, and thousands of "volunteer" troops to

Franco's insurgents. Why? asked Marion. "Don't talk to me about it," replied FDR. "Talk to Cordell Hull." She would love to, she said ("Mr. Hull was my favorite member of the Cabinet"), "but I can't imagine his being the least bit interested in seeing me." "Go call him," ordered the President of the United States. The upshot was that she spent the following morning, a Sunday morning, with Hull (he knew, of course, that her phone call to him had been made at FDR's suggestion), "and we had a long, long talk, and he was very patient, very kind, very nice," as Marion says, but only "reasonably convincing."

FDR also, Marion says, "impressed upon all of us who were close to him that we must keep our good humor, we must keep our tempers, in the face of hostile criticism of him and of the New Deal." This was sometimes very hard for her to do. Few among the parents of Todhunter students were in favor of Roosevelt and the New Deal. Most were bitterly, angrily hostile—"and at one time it was sort of an indoor sport to invite me to dinner, just to bait me about the administration." She remembers particularly a dinner party at which every one of the men joined in a circle around her in the drawing room. "I knew it was not my charm that drew them to me. I was to be the target." But somehow, reminding herself of FDR's injunction, she managed to remain "perfectly cool, perfectly calm" as she answered their attacks. "The next day I received a huge box of flowers, and in it a note from young Frank Vanderlip saying, 'I didn't agree with one single thing you said, but I take off my hat to you for not losing your temper.'"

The only New Deal measures conceded—reluctantly—to be necessary by the men who surrounded Marion on that memorable evening were the Securities Act of 1933 and the Securities Exchange Act of 1934—which reminds Marion how astonished and even outraged she herself was when Roosevelt appointed as the first chairman of the Securities and Exchange Commission (SEC) one of the most notorious speculators and stock price manipulators in America (he had helped organize a Libby-Owens-Ford stock pool as recently as 1933), Joseph P. Kennedy of Boston. "How on earth could you do that?"

asked Marion of the President. He looked at her with a quizzical smile. "Set a thief to catch a thief," he said.

No man in Marion's experience was a better natural raconteur than FDR, and none other had so immense a store of personally lived experience from which to draw true story material. Before the fireplace in the Oval Room of the White House, at the family dining table of that house, on Bowdell's Knob at Warm Springs, in special trains, in the Big House at Hyde Park or on the Val Kill picnic grounds—in each of these places Marion listened to the President's stories. The way in which they began was almost invariably the same. FDR would have his long ivory cigarette holder clamped between his teeth, the cigarette jutting upward at an angle so steep that when he tossed his head back in a characteristic gesture he risked shaking ash into his eyes. His gaze would sweep the group surrounding him, imposing an attentive silence, and he would begin, "Well, as I was saying—" though often the story that followed was apropos of nothing he had just said. He had several favorites that he told over and over again. One of them—it became a favorite of Marion's also—concerned a Catholic priest, who in 1919, when FDR was Assistant Secretary of the Navy and was in France to settle French war claims against the U.S. Navy, was struck down on the street of a Brittany village by a U.S. Navy automobile shortly before FDR arrived there. The priest, a small, elderly man, insisted he was uninjured, but FDR ordered a medical examination anyway (FDR always told how layer after layer of clothing had to be removed) to confirm the fact. When pressed to accept money for his "shock and discomfort," the little priest proudly refused, but when FDR asked if there were anything he wanted for his church, the priest admitted that there was. The stained-glass windows of his sixteenth-century church permitted upon the altar a remarkably beautiful filtered sunlight. The leading of these windows, however, was cracked and broken, so that often pieces of glass dropped out, and he had long wished to have the windows releaded. The price he named for doing this was modest; FDR promptly handed him a check for the specified amount. When the Assistant Secretary left, the little priest called after him: "Always in my church a candle will burn for the Navy of the United States!"

One day in the summer of 1934, Marion had occasion to call at the Wall Street office of a financier friend of hers who seldom failed to express to her his hostility toward Roosevelt and the New Deal. On this occasion he had lying on his deak—lying in wait for Marion, perhaps—a recently published little book entitled *Frankie in Wonderland*, by Latham R. Reed, "A Tory, With Apologies to Lewis Carroll." (Carroll's *Alice in Wonderland*, according to author Reed, was a "prehistory" of the New Deal.) The Wall Street man proceeded to read extracts from this book with great glee and gusto, expecting Marion to protest against the barbs of ridicule shot at FDR. Instead, she asked where she might obtain a copy of the book to present to the President, with whom and whose family she expected to dine that evening in Hyde Park. Her friend stared at her incredulously. "You wouldn't do that!" he said. Yes, she certainly would, said Marion, if only she could get the book. "He'll love it!" she added. Whereupon her disbelieving friend offered her his copy, gratis, provided that she tell him later what the President "*really* said" about it. She promised to do so.

But as things turned out, there was no need for her telling him; within forty-eight hours FDR's response to the book was national news.

Marion presented it to him at the dinner table in the Big House a few hours later, and the delight he immediately took in it was a joy to behold—and to hear. He read the whole of the small volume aloud during the evening; he called for his copy of *Alice*, so that he could check the parody against it (he pronounced the parody witty, the humor delicious). He then announced that on the morrow he would read the entire work to newsmen assembled for the annual picnic he gave them at the Val Kill Cottage picnic ground. (Nancy, as always, was in charge of the food and drink.)

And that is what he did.

130

At the end of a warm afternoon, when "everyone was drained from very much exercise," says Marion, "and after the newspaper people had got their hot dogs from the front of the fireplace, they sat down in a semicircle group around him." Having told them he had "something really good" for them, he took *Frankie in Wonderland* from his pocket and began to read with great expressiveness, histrionically, the story of how Little Frankie, "tired of having only one state to play with," and anxious also to "get rid of the rowdy little Smith boy who always wanted to play with his toys," was inspired by the sight of "the White Rabbit with pink eyes" dashing by him into "a large rabbit hole under the hedge." An idea was born. "What the country really needs, thought Little Frankie, is a few rabbit tricks—and if I could catch a nice white rabbit, particularly one with pink eyes, I could throw my hat into the ring and then pull the rabbit out of the hat, and then I'd have forty-eight states to play with instead of only one. So, without considering how in the world he would ever get out of it again, he popped into the hole after the rabbit." Thus began a carnival of absurdities, each absurdity unmistakably bearing a New Deal tag—and when the carnival ended—though the author asserted that "The End Is Not Yet"—FDR's auditors were limp with laughter.

As the party broke up, Marion happened to be standing next to a new member of the White House press corps, the correspondent of a Midwestern paper that was especially vicious in its attacks upon Roosevelt. This correspondent was muttering to himself in a kind of helpless wonder, "What can you do with a man like that? You can't keep him down, that's sure."

Later, during the 1936 campaign, this same correspondent joined with his colleagues to frustrate the efforts of a news photographer to obtain, on orders from his virulently anti-Roosevelt editor, a picture of Roosevelt being carried, as he sometimes had to be on every campaign day if he were to keep up with his rigorous time schedule. "This editor thought he could use such a picture to discredit the President's capability as a person," says Marion. The newsmen were outraged. "Accidents" plagued the luckless photographer. Sometimes his camera was jostled just as he was taking the ordered shot; sometimes it was actually knocked out of his hands; sometimes his view was blocked at the crucial moment; more often he found that every vantage point from which the picture could be taken had been preempted. For the newsmen went so far as to assign one or another of their number to travel ahead of the campaign party, while they "covered" for him with his home office, so that every spot from which the objectionable shot could be made was located before the campaign train arrived.

"Now, that was the kind of loyalty he [FDR] had from the reporters," says Marion. "I think ninety percent of the editors opposed him [actually, in 1936, he was opposed by approximately eighty percent of the big dailies], but he won virtually one hundred percent of the reporters assigned to the White House. He had an easy, delightful give-and-take relationship with them—was always willing to discuss problems and incidents with them man to man, though without compromising his authority as President of the United States."

FDR had a special interest and a strictly classical-traditionalist taste in architecture, and was inclined to overrate his architectural abilities, in the experienced opinion of Henry Toombs and Eric Gugler, the two professionals in this field with whom he most closely associated. He was also inclined to take credit on occasion for architectural work actually done by Toombs or Gugler, or both together, to their mingled amusement and irritation.

One Wednesday morning, not many months after the Arthurdale prefab housing fiasco, Marion, Nancy, and Eleanor joined the President in the Oval Room of the White House to await the arrival of Gugler for a meeting of importance to governmental architectural history. A week or two before, Gugler, a brilliant, warm, temperamental man, not noted for his tact, had protested to the President, on behalf of the Fine Arts Commission, plans already approved by FDR for enlargement of the Executive Office wing of the White House. The plans were an outrage against both history and architecture, Gugler said. They were a complete departure from Jefferson's careful, tasteful designs for possible future additions to the White House, and they would produce a monstrosity totally destructive of the building's symmetry, flatly contradictory of its basic original design. FDR was annoyed. "People like you care more for appearances than you do about your country's government," he charged, pointing out—and this is a measure of the rare extent of his annoyance—that he was physically handicapped and the lack of adequate working space immediately adjacent to his living quarters added to his already sufficiently great difficulty in "running the government."

A day or two later Gugler returned for a scheduled appointment with a bold suggestion: "If you need, as you say, three times the office space in addition to the major rooms, and I can show that this space can be provided without increasing the apparent size of the building— no change to the eye, as to size—will you consider my plan?" The President looked at him hard. "All right," he said, finally, "come back this coming Wednesday morning [it was then Friday] with drawings. I'll decide then." It was for this meeting that Marion, Nancy, and Eleanor were assembled.

Gugler arrived in a jubilant mood, spread his drawings out on the Oval Room floor, and explained them in rapid-fire talk. "I was positively happy to find Mrs. Roosevelt there, along with her dear friends," said Gugler later. "I have been working with all three of them [on Arthurdale]—and they, too, understood, quite completely I think, the rather complex problems involved." Marion did understand. She knew Eric had done a brilliant job. And she remembers how tense they all grew as they awaited the President's final decision—how joyful they all were when, after a long silent study, the President approved the plans—although he did so with no great show of enthusiasm.*

---

* He shaped a political parable out of this project in a public statement a few days later. He said:

"While I am away from Washington this summer a long-needed renovation of and addition to our White House office building is to be started. The architects have planned a few new rooms built into the present all too small one-story structure. . . . But the structural lines of the White House Buildings will remain. The artistic lines of the White House Buildings were the creation of master builders when our Republic was young. The simplicity and strength of

But when the new building was completed and he was shown through it for the first time, he kept saying proudly, "That I like! That I like!" as if what he saw were the carrying out of his own ideas. His wheelchair was being pushed by Billy Delano, his own relative and Gugler's close friend, and Billy grew annoyed by FDR's seeming obliviousness to Eric Gugler's presence and to the fact that Gugler was the architect. "But Franklin!" Billy protested at last. "Surely that's all Eric's design, and his work, don't you think?" "Oh, yes, yes, of course," FDR said hastily.

If FDR responded irritably to Gugler's abrasiveness, he seldom responded so to anyone else. Remarkable in general was his patient persistence and even-temperedness under pressure, joined to an amazing buoyancy that enabled him to "come bouncing back gaily from the most grievous rebuffs and disappointments."

In this connection, Marion recalls especially her experience of May 27, 1935—the Black Monday of the New Deal, as historians have dubbed it—when she was staying in the White House.

On that day, between noon and midafternoon, the U.S. Supreme Court rendered three unanimous anti-administration decisions. The final one, seemingly totally destructive of the New Deal's approach to government, was the opinion declaring unconstitutional the NRA, cornerstone of the initial New Deal's industrial recovery program.

---

the structure remain in the face of every modern test. But within this magnificent pattern, the necessities of modern government business require constant reorganization and rebuilding.

"If I were to listen to the arguments of some prophets of calamity who are talking these days, I would hesitate to make these alterations. I should fear that while I am away for a few weeks the architects might build some strange new Gothic tower or a factory building or perhaps a replica of the Kremlin or of the Potsdam Palace. But I have no such fears. The architects and builders are men of common sense and artistic American tastes. They know that the principles of harmony and of necessity itself require that the building of the new structure shall blend with the essential lines of the old. It is this combination of the old and new that makes orderly peaceful progress—not only in buildings but in building government itself.

"Our new structure is a part of and a fulfillment of the old."

134

Marion and Eleanor "dreaded going down to dinner that night." They both tried to think of things they might say to cheer up FDR. Great, therefore, was their surprise and relief when at the dinner table he gave no sign of dismay or even minor perturbation. The Supreme Court was not so much as mentioned! Later Marion went into his bedroom, to bid him goodnight. "He was sitting up in bed with his old sweater on, working on his stamps," she remembers. "To all appearances he was perfectly happy and at peace with the world."

Nevertheless, it was Marion's opinion, even at the time, that he was "gathering his forces, mental and physical and spiritual, to meet a very disheartening blow." It is her present conviction that he was making on that bitter day his decision "that the character of the Supreme Court must be changed." This led to his notorious and ill-fated "court-packing scheme," which, says Marion, "troubled me very much because it seemed to me to be going against a very well-founded tradition and smacked a little too much of a smart method of meeting a problem." She said as much to him—to no avail, of course. Nor would he ever admit that he had been mistaken—not even after Congress had rejected his plan emphatically, his popularity (as revealed by the polls) was drastically reduced, and his congressional opposition was so strengthened that the bulk of his legislative program failed of passage. "But the fact that I felt perfectly free to disagree with him altogether on this occasion indicates one of his most outstanding characteristics," says Marion. "He never insisted that you agree with him, even about things to which he was deeply committed, as the price of his continued personal friendship with you. He often encouraged opposing arguments as tests of his own when talking in the bosom of the family. He could disagree with you and accept sharp, strong criticism without loss of his good humor."

Marion remembers one occasion, however, when FDR in a dinner argument at the White House did come close to losing his temper—and the object of his wrath was, of all people, calm, sweet, gentle Caroline O'Day!

In 1934 the New York State Democratic Convention, meeting in

Buffalo, nominated Caroline for congresswoman-at-large. Eleanor came up from Washington to campaign for her friend, making as many as five speeches on her behalf in a single day, provoking loud outcry in the Republican press. Nancy and Marion also worked hard for Caroline. And on election day Caroline won by a large majority. She won again in 1936, 1938, and 1940, having established herself as one of the most effective and influential liberals in the House, a staunch supporter of the President on virtually every major legislative proposal. But she remained an ardent, uncompromising pacifist. In 1939, when Hitler's Germany, Mussolini's Italy, and militaristic Japan were on the march toward world conquest, she was as firmly committed to American neutrality—that is, to an isolationist foreign policy—as she had been in 1917. FDR strove desperately, in the early summer of 1939, for a bill that would repeal the compulsory embargo provisions of the Neutrality Act, so that he might have some slight flexibility of response to the aggressive threats of Nazi Germany. Caroline O'Day opposed this bill.

It was in an effort to persuade her to cease such opposition that FDR invited Caroline to dine at the White House on the occasion Marion so vividly remembers. They sat long at table that night, Marion listening with the closest attention to what became an argument between the congresswoman and the President of the United States, "whom she [Caroline] loved" as a friend. FDR argued that passage of the embargo repeal would lessen the likelihood of a new world war. The bill was a peace measure, not a war measure; failure to pass it "would weaken the leadership of the United States in exercising its potent influence in the cause of preserving peace," as the President would put it in a public statement a few weeks later. Caroline argued that passage of the bill would increase the likelihood of American involvement in the world war now threatened—would, in fact, make such involvement virtually a certainty if the war came, since the President would then embargo shipments to Nazi Germany but not to England and France. "They talked and talked and talked." FDR became heated, snappish. Caroline "never lost her calm, nor her firmness."

Finally, near midnight, the President broke off the discussion. He turned to Marion who, he knew, stood on his side of this argument, and he ordered her rather grimly to go home with Caroline and spend the night "and try to make her see reason." Marion did as he asked, of course, "but I knew that I could do nothing to change Caroline's mind on this, which was a matter of absolute principle with her. I achieved nothing. In the following year Caroline voted against the Selective Service Bill."

On a Friday afternoon in April 1940, Marion arrived at the White House to spend a weekend. There were a few other guests for dinner that evening, and as often happened, all were asked to join the President in his study, the Oval Room, for predinner cocktails. Marion arrived in the study earlier than the others to find FDR "sitting behind a great table desk, strewn with papers, maps, pictures, books," and a clutter of miscellaneous objects. (Among these last was a cloth elephant, symbol of the Republican party. "I remember Missy's telling about that elephant," says Marion. "It was made of some material that got awfully dirty. Missy had it dry-cleaned several times, and every time she did it would shrink some more. This delighted Franklin. 'It's coming down to natural size,' he said.") He was in one of his raconteur moods, that late afternoon. He ran his hand rather lovingly over the top of his desk, which was, he told her, the historic *Resolute* desk. "You know its history, of course?" he asked. She confessed she didn't, provoking a chiding for her "dearth of historical information."

He then proceeded to recount how, in 1845, Sir John Franklin sailed from England in command of two ships with 134 men, in search of the long-sought-after Northwest Passage (". . . I resolved that when I was next in London I would pay a visit to Sir John's monument in Westminster Abbey," says Marion). The last sighting of the ships was by a whaler in Baffin Bay in July of 1845. No great anxiety was felt for two years thereafter, but between 1848 and 1854 no fewer than fifteen rescue expeditions were sent out by both England and the United States. There was no rescue; Franklin and his men were forever lost.

All this was reviewed by FDR in succinct detail. Then he read to Marion the inscription of the plaque mounted on the front of the desk drawer:

"HMS *Resolute*, forming part of the expedition sent in search of Sir John Franklin in 1852, was abandoned in Latitude 74 degrees, 41 minutes North, on May 15, 1852. She was discovered and extracted on September 10, 1855, by Captain George Bennington of the U.S. ship, the whaler *George Henry*. The ship was purchased, fitted out and sent to England as a gift to Her Majesty Queen Victoria by the President and the people of the United States as a token of good will and friendship. This table was made from her timbers, when she was broken up, and was presented by the Queen of Great Britain and Ireland to the President of the United States, as a memorial to the courtesy and loving kindness which dictated the offer of the *Resolute*."

The other guests entered the Oval Room as FDR finished reading the inscription, and to all of them he explained that one of his first requests on coming to the White House had been to have this table brought up to his study from the basement, where it had been stored. "Sailor that he was," according to Marion, "it meant much to him to have a desk fraught with such memories on which to do his work."

On Sunday night she returned to New York City. At school assembly next morning she told her students about the *Resolute* desk. One of these students, a senior, collected historical inscriptions as a hobby. "When she asked me for a copy of the *Resolute* desk inscription, I readily promised to secure an accurate one for her the next time I was in Washington," says Marion.

She was not again in the White House for a weekend until mid-May.

In that month of that year, the springtime brightness was darkened by rising clouds of war. There was in Washington a thickening gloom of anxiety as Hitler's Nazi hordes raged down through the Low Countries into a doomed France. There was much talk of espionage and counterespionage: Marion was told of tightened security measures being taken by the FBI and the Secret Service.

138

There was an actual physical gloom on the second floor of the White House in the late afternoon of Sunday, as Marion awaited the time when she must board her train for New York. The sky was overcast. Marion, the only house guest, was alone in the Roosevelt family quarters, for both the President and Eleanor had gone out.

Suddenly she remembered the promise she had given her student. Time being short, she hurried down the corridor to the Oval Room. Its door was open. She entered, pushed the President's chair away from the desk, sat down on the floor where the chair had been so that her eyes were level with the plaque, and began hastily to copy the inscription. The light was bad. She pulled out the drawer a quarter-inch, so that she might read more easily. Even then she had difficulty, so she struck several matches, one after another, to light the plaque until the copying was done. She dropped the burnt matches into the wastebasket beside the desk, and suitcase in hand, went down to the White House limousine, which took her to the station.

Next morning Marion's secretary, typing the inscription, had difficulty with two or three of the hastily copied words, so Marion sent the typescript to Tommy, Eleanor's secretary, asking that it be checked. Tommy wrote back very promptly, returning the corrected typescript and informing Marion of "the uproar" which her "desire . . . to collect historical data" had caused in the White House.

For when the Secret Service men inspected the Oval Room before the President reentered it and found that his chair was pushed aside, that a drawer containing top-secret documents was slightly open, and that burnt matches were in the wastebasket, they sharply questioned the man responsible for the study's housekeeping. He swore that everything had been in order when he last saw the room. The desk, which had been wiped with an oiled dustcloth after the President left, was then dusted for fingerprints, of which some were discovered; all the White House personnel were fingerprinted. And when it was found that the prints on the desk matched none just taken, nor any on file in the FBI, concern mounted to great anxiety. The President himself grew worried.

Then came Marion's letter, explaining all. There was great relief but also, pardonably, a measure of irritation with Marion.

Next time she was in the White House, the President spoke to her with unwonted sternness. "Marion," said he, "I have made an appointment for you with the FBI tomorrow morning. You are going to be fingerprinted." She inferred, because he clearly implied, that the order stemmed from her transgression in May. She protested. "I knew I shouldn't have done what I had done," she says, "but it didn't seem to me justification for having me fingerprinted and indexed with the nation's criminals. I begged him not to do it, promising that I would never go near anything that belonged to him again as long as I lived. He merely said, 'Your appointment is at 10 o'clock. Please keep it.' "

The fingerprinting, in those circumstances, was a deep humiliation for her. "I was crushed." And humiliation was compounded when, the prints taken, she was asked to wait for a few minutes until her "card" could be prepared. "Do I have to wear a card, too?" she burst out.

Not until then did she learn that what she was undergoing was not a punishment for the May episode.

"Your property at Hyde Park is surrounded by the President's," the FBI told her, "and everyone going back and forth there must be fingerprinted and carry a card, for identification by personnel."

She was "relieved but a bit angry with the President" as she took her card and returned to the White House.

"He never let me forget that," she says. "He enjoyed this kind of practical joke. . . . I remember how he told over and over again, in Louis Howe's presence, how Louis, when he ran Franklin's 1912 campaign for the state senate, added up the amounts on check stubs instead of subtracting them, and reported as a result that there was a healthy balance in the bank when in fact the account was overdrawn. He was warm and kind, but he did have this little streak which made him rather enjoy seeing people squirm now and then."

140

T W E L V E

WHEN the *Resolute*-desk episode occurred, Louis had been dead four years.

Nearly two years had passed since a sad, drastic change came over the personal relationship between Eleanor and her theretofore closest friends.

The two events—Howe's death and the near death of a rare friendship—are joined, as Marion recognizes in her retrospective view.

Howe, under the stimulus of the realization of his great dream, made a remarkable recovery in the fall and winter of 1932 from his nearly fatal collapse at the time of the Chicago convention. He moved in March of 1933 into a bedroom opening off the Lincoln room in the White House, across the hall from Eleanor's sitting room; and for a year and more thereafter he operated at his highest pitch, riding a

141

burst of energy that was like the last upward surge of flame before the match burns out. He seems to have known, deep down, that the end was near. The reckless haste of his launching of the Reedsville project, the irritable impatience of which many complained who dealt with him on public business, the short shrift he gave those who sought to cultivate his personal acquaintance solely and simply because he was secretary to the President—all these are accounted for by his realization that he had, literally, no time to waste. No time at all.

In the fall of 1934 he began visibly to fail. Breathing became more difficult, his ghastly coughing spells more frequent, his thin body thinner still. He spent more and more time in his room, sitting in pajamas and robe amid a clutter of newspapers, typescript, and documents, conducting an increasing amount of his business by phone. Marion remembers how he tottered in dressing gown into Eleanor's sitting room one day when she was there and how deathly ill he looked with his great eyes burning feverishly in the sockets of a skeletal face. In January of 1935 he was bedridden—far too ill to plan and organize the annual Cuff Links Club dinner, which was canceled that year—and two months later he went into a coma. Eleanor wrote, sadly, to Molly Dewson, organizer of national Democratic campaigns, that though he "seems to cling to life in the most astonishing manner, . . . I am afraid the end is near." He came out of the coma, however, living on for another year, most of it in the Naval Hospital in Washington, much of it under an oxygen tent, his mind teeming with political ideas and plans for the upcoming 1936 presidential campaign, though he confessed to one visitor his realization that he himself could have no part in that campaign. "Franklin is on his own now," he whispered.

He died on April 18, 1936, aged sixty-five.

He was sorely missed. "Louis Howe's death left a great gap in my husband's life," Eleanor writes in *This I Remember*. "I have always felt that if Louis had lived the number of people drawn closely but briefly into the working and social orbits of Franklin's life would have been fewer. For one reason and another, no one quite filled the void which he was unconsciously seeking to fill. . . . There are not many

142

men in this world whose personal ambition it is to accomplish things for someone else, and it was some time before a friendship with Harry Hopkins, somewhat different but similar in certain ways, again brought Franklin some of the satisfaction he had known with Louis Howe."*

Most grievous for those of the innermost family circle was the loss of Howe as a vital link between Eleanor and the President—as the sole means, in some instances, for their sympathetic working communication with one another. He had been a very dear *mutual* friend. Eleanor loved and trusted him totally. So did FDR. So, to the extent of their involvement with him, did Marion and Nancy. And this had made of him a stabilizing, humanizing, ameliorative influence: it had enabled his sensitive mind and empathic sympathy—which belied the harsh, irascible self he so often showed "outsiders"—to smooth many a rough passage and block many a tendency toward quarrel and dissolution among the Roosevelt intimates.

The need for such influence, so far as the relations between Eleanor and Marion and Nancy were concerned, grew during the long months of Howe's fatal illness—and became acute during the months that followed.

Inevitably, after and because of Eleanor's elevation—however reluctantly—to the White House, possibilities of misunderstanding were multiplied between Eleanor and her two friends. The blazing light of publicity that focused upon her as First Lady magnified the importance of her role in every undertaking of which she was, or had been, a part; and her two friends would have been less than human had they not regarded a bit wryly, on occasion, the newspaper and magazine articles that identified Todhunter as "Mrs. Roosevelt's school" and Val-Kill Industries as "Mrs. Roosevelt's furniture-making project." (Actually, as Eleanor realized, her association with the school became a dubious economic asset when animosity toward FDR and the New

---

* It is notable that Hopkins in his years of closest association with FDR was incapacitated for the pursuit of purely personal ambitions by his physical condition, as Howe had been.

Deal grew virulent on the part of the affluent from whom Todhunter's enrollment was largely drawn.)

More important was the fact that Eleanor was now necessarily involved more and more in activities in which it was impossible for her, though she often tried, to involve or even much interest her long-time friends. She necessarily enlarged greatly her circle of acquaintances, of whom many became personal friends, and often these new friends of hers remained strangers to Nancy and Marion—a marked change from former days, when a friend of any one of the three became the friend of all. A result of these developments was that interests that had formerly been central and major in Eleanor's life, and which perforce remained so in the lives of Marion and Nancy—the Cottage, Val-Kill Shop, Todhunter, the Women's Division of the state Democratic party— became for Eleanor peripheral, relatively minor.

Coincident with the changes in circumstance was Eleanor's continuing growth toward true inward independence. She no longer leaned emotionally on Nancy and Marion, as she had formerly done. In earlier years she had largely followed their initiatives in joint enterprises, and gratefully. Now she operated for the most part upon her own initiatives. A happy continuation of the relationship required, therefore, radical attitudinal adjustments and new accommodations among the three, or between one of them and the other two—and these were difficult to make. They were perhaps especially so for Nancy. She was closer to Eleanor than Marion was; she grew more and more weary under the Arthurdale burden she had assumed, at Eleanor's behest, in addition to those of the Women's Division and shop.

And all this was enhanced, as a hazard to friendship, by what Eleanor herself recognized as the least endearing of all her psychological traits.

When hurt, instead of letting the cause and nature of her hurt be known, she was inclined to withdraw into a cave of silence, "feeling like a martyr and acting like one," as she confessed, emerging only after she had raised around her injured feelings walls that were as cold and hard and impenetrable as iron. She then often continued to refuse to communicate on the subject of her hurt with whomever had hurt her. This could be psychologically devastating to the other person, in proportion to the other's caring for her: it raised up in the other's bosom—it was designed to do so, if unconsciously—a fifth column of anxieties, doubts, fears, and guilt feelings that could overwhelm from within. Eleanor's White House circumstances enabled her to operate in this way with less empathic awareness of the effect she was producing, hence with more ruthlessness, than ever before, since these circumstances provided her with a greater abundance of attention-diverting and -absorbing objects than she had theretofore known.

Simultaneous with the dying of Louis Howe through the early months of 1936 was the dying of the Val-Kill furniture enterprise; and just one month after Howe's published obituary came the obituary of the shop.

According to "an announcement made by Mrs. Franklin D. Roosevelt," the shop at Hyde Park "will be taken over and operated by one of the expert craftsmen, Otto Berge, of East Park, New York." So said a news release dated Thursday, May 14, the release going on to say that "Miss Nancy Cook, President of Val-Kill, who has conducted the shop since its founding, finds the various craft projects have grown to such an extent that she can no longer give them her personal attention. . . . The weaving will continue under the direction of Nellie Johannesen. During the winter months she will teach the art of weaving to any women who wish to learn."*

The dry, matter-of-fact words told nothing of the heartache this meant to Nancy Cook, who had invented this enterprise and for whom it had been the center, the essence of creative self-expression. She continued in the following months to make items with shop equipment, or to have them made under her supervision by Otto Berge, or Arnold

---

* In point of fact, the three co-owners *gave* the machinery to Berge, who moved it into the shop he had behind his house. The pewter-making equipment was given Arnold Berge, a relative of Otto's, and the weaving equipment was given to Nellie Johannesen.

Berge, in fulfillment of White House orders—gifts for birthdays and weddings, souvenirs of special occasions, and the like. But the fashioning of such relatively trivial items was no substitute for the former furniture-making, and the fact that the requests for 1937 were made through a social secretary (Mrs. Edith Bentham Helm) instead of directly by Eleanor indicates the distance now being opened—partly by the pressures on Eleanor's time, partly for other and inward reasons—between her and her two friends.

The distance widened. Eleanor proposed in late 1936 or early 1937 that she take over the shop building and transform it into her very own country home. She had plausible, obvious reasons for such a proposal: she needed a place of her own, a Val Kill house, in which activities and people having no part in Marion's life, or Nancy's, could be entertained without disturbing their lives. But her removal from the cottage did mean a loosening of ties, which Marion and Nancy could not but regret. The old days, with the three of them in the cottage, had been so rich in experience, so glowing with loving friendship, so gloriously happy on the whole! Nancy made or supervised the making of all the new furniture for Eleanor's new home, but Eleanor indicated that she did not wish Nancy to do more than that. In a revealing letter of May 26, 1937, she told "Dear Nan" that she wanted the furniture "stood aside as finished until I arrive. . . . I don't want anything moved into place until I am there to direct it. I will be there Friday afternoon and through the day Saturday. . . ." This was a new departure. In former years it would have been taken for granted that Nan would manage all the moving, earning thereby expressions of gratitude from Eleanor. And that same letter went on to indicate the growing separation of Eleanor from the work of the Women's Division for which Nancy, as executive secretary, was responsible. "Do you really think it absolutely necessary, and will you please ask Agnes [Mrs. Henry Goddard Leach], for me, whether it will upset her if I did not appear at that afternoon meeting in Syracuse [?]" wrote Eleanor. "It would be much easier for me, though I can make it if necessary."

During this same period and the year following there was also a

146

growing separation of Eleanor from the work of the Todhunter School.

It coincided with the trials and vicissitudes of Marion's program for expanding the school—a program that led to disappointment as grievous to her as the loss of the shop had been to Nancy. The first step was to acquire a new building, since the one at 66 East Eightieth Street was inadequate even for the present enrollment, and in early January of 1937 it appeared that the acquisition might be quite easily made. One of Todhunter's pupils was the niece of Bernard Baruch, who offered to help financially and otherwise with the purchase of a house that was admirably suited to the school's needs. Greatly excited, Marion promptly informed Eleanor, then in the midst of the preparations for her husband's second inaugural. "I am thrilled to hear about your talk with Mr. Baruch and the offer which he made," Eleanor replied on January 13. "I shall hold my breath until I hear the results!"

One week later (January 20, 1937), Nancy and Marion were guests in the White House on inauguration day. As in 1933, Nancy stayed on for several days. She was there when Marion wrote from New York to Eleanor saying that the "inauguration and all the events associated with it were far more than interesting to me and out of it all came many associations and memories that will stay with me forever." She went on to say that the sale price of the selected house "is definitely $102,500."

Two or three days later she wrote Eleanor: "Mr. Baruch has just called me and told me that he was leaving the matter with Harry Hooker [former law partner of FDR] and that he could have the building for $100,000." In a handwritten note below this typewritten epistle, Marion wrote, "I am terribly thrilled and hope you are a little bit too!"

But then arose a serious difficulty, perhaps an impossibility, of obtaining the clear title to the building, upon which all financial arrangements depended. Marion told Eleanor all about it on Sunday evening, February 7, in Val Kill Cottage, and wrote to her next day: "I was sorry to have to tell you so much in so short a time. . . . Should I have good news before the day is over I will telegraph you." Handwritten below her signature was: "At the moment I am a bit low!" There was no telegram, and on February 10 Eleanor wrote back: "I know how low you are feeling and only hope everything will come out all right. . . . I am terribly sorry that you must be held up when I know just how anxious you are and how trying it is not to have things settled."

Clearly Eleanor no longer identified with the school as she had said she intended to do in her *New York Times Magazine* interview of late 1932. The school is Marion's, the problem of its expansion is Marion's, and all Eleanor can do is offer sympathy, at Marion's request, a modicum of help.

The impasse, with regard to the building purchase, continued into the autumn. From Chicago on November 7, 1937, Eleanor wrote Marion about a report on Todhunter curriculum joined with a proposed fund-raising campaign for the school's expansion, which Marion had sent her. She made a few corrections and several suggestions concerning a postgraduate course she herself had suggested. On that same day she sent the report to FDR, saying: "Will you look at this? I have turned down the pages and marked such places as I think you should read. I confess I think this is a tremendous task and wish I could be as optimistic as they [Marion and Nancy] are! However, if the market goes up it may not be so bad." Her basic feeling, revealed to her husband but never to Marion or Nancy, was that the wise thing would be for her to withdraw altogether from the Todhunter enterprise.

Her doubts grew. In early March of 1938, when a Todhunter fund-raising brochure was being prepared by a professional in such matters, Eleanor, on request, contributed a statement to it. The brochure editor sought to strengthen it by having her say that she intended to make Todhunter again a major interest of hers when she left the White House. "I am terribly sorry," she wrote back, "but as I do not intend to make the school one of my major interests, I feel it very much wiser to be absolutely honest. It will be one of my interests, but as I have no definite idea of what my other interests will be or where they will take me, I regret that I cannot change my statement." Some weeks later, on April 28, she wrote Harry Hooker frankly of her relief that the expansion program was being laid aside, for the time being, due to the sharp recession that had begun in the early fall of 1937 and yet continued.

In the late spring of 1938 FDR appointed Marion one of the two women members of a nine-member President's Commission to Study Industrial Relations in Great Britain and Sweden—a commission whose chairman was Gerard Swope of General Electric. She sailed for England on the S.S. *Washington* on June 28; and on the night before she left Hyde Park she had a long talk with Eleanor about Todhunter and Val Kill. "At that time I knew we had some problems ahead," Marion later wrote, "but not ones that seemed impossible of solution." They bid an affectionate good-bye to one another, and Eleanor sent to Marion's ship cabin, as bon voyage gifts, flowers and a check. Several letters as affectionate in tone as ever were exchanged between the two while Marion was abroad.

The commission toured industrial establishments in England and Sweden, then crossed from Sweden to Hamburg, where Marion phoned Nancy. Nancy was her usual self on the phone; all was well. From Hamburg the commissioners came down by train through Hitler's Germany toward France. There was an ugly, anxious moment in Germany when the commissioners were told that Nazi officials would board the train at the next stop to examine passports, and Gerard Swope, who was a Jew, could not find his in his luggage. He finally did so in the nick of time ("—it's the only time I ever saw Mr. Swope absolutely harassed, undone," Marion remembers). It was an experience that reduced Swope's tolerance, which would have been severely limited in any case, of views expressed by Joseph P. Kennedy, then Ambassador to Great Britain, during an Embassy luncheon he gave the commissioners when they passed through London on their return trip. Kennedy had great sympathy and admiration for Adolf Hitler, great antipathy and contempt for certain features of English and American life, and he said so forcefully, crudely. Swope's face was hardened in cold fury as he pressed into the hand of Marion, who was his table companion, a note saying, "In five minutes you and I are leaving this table." Marion would have liked to do so but "I knew we shouldn't because we were not there as individuals but as representatives of our government, and if we made a scene it would have been a disservice to the government." She indicated as much to Swope, who was forced to agree with her, "and so we stayed, but it was an unhappy time and left a very unpleasant feeling in my mind in regard to Mr. Kennedy."

It was when the ship on which the commission returned docked in New York on August 18 that Marion had her first sharp awareness that a great and unhappy change was being made in her personal life. And Nancy's. Nancy was at the dock. Marion will never forget the shock of her meeting with her friend.

Nancy's face was drawn and paler than Marion had ever seen it; her eyelids were red and swollen with weeping. In response to Marion's quick, anxious questioning, she achieved only a tearful incoherence from which Marion extracted the single solid fact that Nancy and Eleanor had had, a week or two before, "a long and tragic talk," during which each of the two "had said things that ought not to have been said," as Marion puts it.

Precisely what those things were, Marion could not learn from Nancy, even after the two had been some days in Val Kill Cottage and Nancy had grown calmer. "It only seemed to make matters worse for Nan when I questioned her," says Marion. Nor could she learn from Eleanor, who refused to see her—Eleanor was now always "too busy" —while tacitly insisting upon a preservaton of appearances so far as the trio's relationship was concerned.

In September, just a month after Marion's return, there was a large picnic at the cottage. Among those present, in addition to Eleanor and the President, were Missy, Caroline O'Day, Dr. Herman Baruch (Bernard Baruch's brother), Hall Roosevelt (Eleanor's younger brother), and Hall's only living son, Danny (Henry was by then a

150

suicide), a boy of twelve or so years. Outwardly it was a typical Roosevelt picnic, full of laughter, loud talk, and boisterous activity. But beneath this bright and cheerful surface was a bitter darkness for Marion and Nancy, and out of it flashed a jagged, cutting ugliness before the evening ended, sparked by the fact that Hall Roosevelt was drinking heavily, as he very often did in those days, and that Eleanor was fiercely, maternally protective of him.* He was so drunk on this autumn night that he hardly knew what he was doing when, playing with his son, he lifted and threw the boy hard against the ground in what was known at Val Kill as "Marion's garden." Danny cried out in pain. Dr. Baruch, examining him, declared his collarbone broken. Missy phoned the hospital in Poughkeepsie to alert the emergency ward while Hall, dismayed and somewhat sobered by what he had done, insisted upon driving the boy himself to the hospital. Whereupon Danny, understandably frightened, begged Marion to go with him. She did, though she was frightened, too, with good reason, for Hall drove them into a ditch as they were leaving the grounds. Fortunately the accident injured no one and was witnessed by a state trooper, who then took over and drove them into Poughkeepsie. The depth of that evening's misery for Marion was reached while she was still at the hospital: Eleanor phoned her there and talked to her "in a way I had never heard before"—abusively, in cold accusatory fury—blaming her for all that had happened ("she reported to the others at the cottage that it was I who had driven into the ditch"), so that Marion, when she returned to the cottage, was utterly crushed. She went up to her room. Soon Missy came to her there. The President wanted her to know, said Missy, that *he* knew that it was Hall, not Marion, who had driven into the ditch. The state trooper had told him.

"The President doesn't want you to be hurt," said Missy.

---

* After a young manhood of brilliant promise, Hall by the mid-1930s had gone far down the road traveled by his and Eleanor's alcoholic father, Elliott. "Oh, he was sad, so very sad!" said Marion. "He had such charm, and great intelligence, and he just wasted it all!"

151

But of course she *was* hurt. Deeply, terribly hurt. And the hurt increased in the following months when Eleanor continued to refuse her a personal interview on this matter or any other.

She, Eleanor, was now determined to dissolve what had initially been established as a lifetime property arrangement among the three friends. She wanted an absolutely clear, exclusive legal title to the shop building. She proposed to give up, in payment for this, her share of Val Kill Cottage and of the Todhunter School reserve fund, in which all three had pooled their school profits for several years in order to finance future expansion. Practical and legal problems of some complexity arose from this; Eleanor refused to discuss them with Marion personally. She insisted, instead, that everything be handled through lawyer Harry Hooker—an insistence that necessarily led, however, to a considerable written correspondence, portions of which are psychologically revealing.

"If you will look back," wrote Eleanor from the White House to Nancy and Marion on October 29, 1938, "I think you will realize that in all our relationship I have never before wanted anything, nor suggested anything about the cottage or the school, and therefore it is entirely natural that we have had no difficulties in previous years. This was quite easy for me because I had no objection to acceding to your wishes." In the present case, however, she went on, she had "a distinct preference and as you do not care to handle it in the way I wish, I have decided to turn over to you now, instead of at my death, my entire interest in the cottage, the shop building and the other buildings, exclusive of the stable which was built entirely with my money. . . . In view of what has happened I feel that I wish also to withdraw entirely from the school. I will give you both with great pleasure my share of the school fund which has been held in my name and on which I have paid income tax every year.* [This was in reply to Marion's contention that the reserve fund was a school trust and not personal property.] I do not expect you to take my name off the letterhead this

* So had Marion and Nancy, of course.

year if that will cause you any embarrassment. I am sure, however, that you will prosper better without any connection with the name, just as I feel the crafts will prosper better if it is understood that they are not in any way tied up with the name of Roosevelt." In the future she would "only come to Hyde Park when the President is at the big house and I will stay at the big house."

Marion and Nancy of course resisted this aggressive martyrdom, this killing generosity.

A telegram went from Marion to Eleanor:

CAN NOT OUR YEARS OF CLOSE ASSOCIATION HELP US AT SUCH A TIME? WE ARE WILLING TO MEET YOU AND ANY AGREEMENT WHICH YOU ALL WORK OUT FOR OUR INTEREST AT HYDE PARK. I AND I ALONE CANNOT INVOLVE IN SUCH A SETTLEMENT INTEREST WHICH IS NOT FULLY MINE AND IS TO BE AT LEAST IN A SENSE A TRUST. PLEASE HELP ME DO THE RIGHT THING.

To which Eleanor replied by wire:

VERY SORRY EVERY MINUTE TODAY IS FILLED. IF YOU WILL ASK NAN TO TELL YOU OF CONVERSATION WITH HER LAST SUMMER THAT SHOULD MAKE EVERYTHING CLEAR. LEAVING EVERY-THING IN HARRY'S HANDS.

On November 6 Marion wrote to Harry Hooker. "With very great reluctance, Nan and I today talked with the President about the problem presented by Eleanor's letters," she said. ". . . he suggests the following solution in regard to financial payment [for the shop building], namely that all furniture in the cottage which is jointly owned and all furniture in the 'shop' which is jointly owned become a part of the real property. . . . In other words the 'shop' building and all jointly owned furniture within it shall be considered as 'shop' property and shall belong to Eleanor exclusively during her lifetime; and the cottage and all jointly owned furniture within it shall be considered as cottage property and shall belong to Nan and me, or to the survivor, exclusively during our lives, or the life of the survivor." Marion and Nancy wished to follow this suggestion.

Eleanor, however, did not.

". . . I will only live in the shop building if there is a tangible settlement of the cash values involved according to Nancy's accounts," she wrote Marion on November 9. "I have made this perfectly clear to both of you over a long period, and last summer I had a talk with Nan. She may not have told you that at that time I told her, that for a long period of time I had been conscious of the fact that we three viewed certain things in very different ways. She told me, for instance, that while we were working in the committee, in the school, and in the industries together, you had both always felt that whatever was done was done for the sole purpose of building me up. My whole conception was entirely different. I went into the industries because I felt that Nan was fulfilling something which she had long wanted to do. I would never have done it alone. I had neither the knowledge nor the background nor the interest.

"I went into the school because I had an interest in education and in young people and being fond of you I was anxious to help you in what you wanted to do. It gave me an opportunity for regular work which I was anxious to have. I went into the political work because Louis was anxious to have me do something to keep up Franklin's interest in a field which he eventually hoped Franklin would return to. I had no personal ambitions of any kind and I have none today.

"Nan told me that all my friends sensed a great difference in me and many of them felt a change in attitude just as you and she felt it. This is probably true and I am free to say that I also have felt a change."

On that same day Eleanor sent Marion a letter resigning from the school. Marion, perforce, accepted it, and through Hooker a financial settlement acceptable to Eleanor was worked out. Thereafter, through the remainder of 1938 and the early part of 1939 there were no personal communications between Eleanor and Marion.

Then, in May of 1939, there was correspondence concerning the problem of removing Eleanor's name from certain Todhunter promo-

154

tional booklets already printed. In a longhand letter dated May 16, Marion wrote sadly: "Since I returned [from the 1938 trip to Europe] I have never had a chance to talk to you about anything. The only instance in which I am conscious of having displeased you was on the night I went to the hospital with Danny. My judgment in that instance may not have been wise. My motive however was a kindly one. I have never understood why you spoke to me that night as you did. Your letter telling me to see Harry Hooker seemed like a bad dream. Three times I asked to see you in order to talk matters over. Each time you refused. I know nothing of what has brought this on my head save the incident to which I refer, and that, unless far more was implicated than I know of, seems rather out of proportion to all that went before."

Eleanor replied in a typewritten letter on May 17, saying in part:

"What you did for Danny that night . . . was not what called forth my displeasure. I was displeased because you did not let me know that Hall had reached a point where this could happen. I, of course, realize that probably not being familiar with gentlemen under those conditions except under different circumstances, you did not realize what was happening. It might have been possible for me to prevent Hall taking the car had I known in time. That would at least have obviated the danger that the situation in the ditch caused, or anything else which might have occurred had you got beyond the ditch."

She referred again, with obvious resentment, to her "long and illuminating talk with Nan" in which she was "made . . . [to] realize that you and Nan felt that you had spent your lives building me up." She had been "a little appalled to discover what was in Nan's mind, and of course must have been in yours," she said. ". . . in addition, on a number of occasions Nan has told me how extremely difficult my name made the school situation for you. You have told me that in spite of that, you wished me to continue my connection because we had begun together. However, in view of the fact that other factors have entered into the situation which made me feel that we no longer had the same relationship that I thought we had had in the past, there was no point in subjecting you to a situation which was detrimental.

155

One real factor was that certain things came back to me through Franklin which made me realize many things which I had never realized before." She was sure, she said, "that we can have a very pleasant and agreeable relationship at Hyde Park" in the future and could "all enjoy many things" together there, "but not on the same basis that we had in the past." Of course, "any work I do in the future will . . . be along entirely different lines which will not bring me into close contact with either of you in your work." Equally of course she would always wish "both you and Nan well in whatever you undertake."

Marion could hardly have been expected to let this go unanswered. A decent self-respect compelled her prompt reply, and she made it in a longhand letter that became the very last of her truly intimate communications with Eleanor Roosevelt.

She wrote:

"After reading your letter I feel that there are two things which I want to make clear.

"First I was no part of your talk & Nan's last summer and feel that I should be allowed to speak for myself. I do not know where this 'building up' idea came from and never heard anyone use the expression before this summer except Louis, then I did not think of it seriously. I have never used the expression nor entertained the idea. I have been busy as you know with the school & have put all that I have to put into anything into it & I thought of your connection in the same way.

"I have always been perfectly frank about what helped and what made at times matters difficult. I have never needed anyone to speak for me.

"I know nothing of what came back to you from Franklin. I talked with him for a few moments one Sunday after you had for a second time refused to talk to me. I made with him two points & two only—the same I made with Harry Hooker. First, the school had no connection with the set up of affairs at Hyde Park; and two, that if you wished to give up everything at Hyde Park because of Nan & me my desire was no less strong and I should prefer to withdraw entirely than to be subjected to the situation I found on my return. I have tried to play fair but at times it seems hard to know what 'fair' means.

"I have accepted your decision in regard to the school but I think that when I start after June 2nd on my own I would rather try to do it on a basis of understanding that can not be misinterpreted & therefore after rereading the booklets I should rather start anew—there is too much expressed in them that might be considered as material that should not be used in the light of what has happened.

"Unless you wish to refer to this matter again I shall consider it closed for I have found nothing in it but disillusionment and unhappiness.

"Needless to say that I shall always wish you success in what ever you may care to do.

Affectionately,
Marion"

And by this the matter was indeed closed, so far as communications between Eleanor and Nancy or Marion were concerned. It was never referred to again.

THIRTEEN

ON THE SURFACE, in those appearances snatched out of living time and held for Marion's later viewing by Nancy's expert photography, the Roosevelt years continued much the same as before.

Even in the early summer of 1939, when Eleanor's Val Kill cottage and the original cottage, though physically only a stone's toss apart, were separated by a psychological distance so great that the very amenities of neighborliness were attenuated by it—even then the two friends remained involved, as part of the inner circle, in Roosevelt family concerns. When the King and Queen of England visited Hyde Park in June, for instance, and were famously entertained at FDR's newly built Hilltop Cottage,* a mile and a half up the hill from Val

* Marion says that FDR's building of Hilltop Cottage was strongly opposed by Granny and that, to Marion's knowledge, he never spent a night there. He

Kill Cottage, Marion and Nancy were invited to meet the royal couple; and Nancy's motion pictures were the only photographs made of it, for all news photographers were barred. (Eleanor, introducing the two to the King, mentioned their service in the Endell Street Hospital during World War I. The King "was most gracious and talked to us a bit about that," Marion remembers.) And as the summer wore on, darkened by the shadow of approaching World War II, a shadow in which purely private concerns shrank toward insignificance, the psychological, social distance between the two Val Kill households was somewhat lessened.

When an offer came that summer to Marion for a merging of Todhunter with the Dalton School, with Marion to become Dalton's associate principal, she told Eleanor of it. She felt free to address to Eleanor in the White House, on September 25, after she had accepted the affiliation offer, a longhand letter in which she said: ". . . Miss Helen Parkhurst [the Dalton principal] and I are planning to come to Washington on Wednesday, October 25th, and if we may spend that night in the White House it will be fine. Then Thursday morning we will drive to Arthurdale. . . . I shall appreciate your suggestions for I want this to be . . . a basis for the [Dalton] seniors trip in the spring." Eleanor replied on September 27: "It will be perfectly all right for you to be here the night of October 25th. I have told both Mrs. Nesbitt and Mr. Crim and they will be looking for you." She gave advice about what to see and do at Arthurdale. "I hope your trip will be successful and that you will have good weather," she closed.

Nancy and Marion continued to exchange gifts with Eleanor at Christmas and on birthdays, continued as members of the Cuff Links Club, continued to be invited to presidential functions and as overnight guests in the White House, continued in the tripartite upkeep of the Val Kill grounds and pool, and became much involved with the Roose-

---

had solemnly promised his mother that he would not. "The big house was his home, Granny insisted. But he loved Hilltop, from which there was a magnificent view of the hills, and would have luncheons there. And tea parties." Some of the furniture for Hilltop was made by Nancy.

velts' informal entertainment of exiled royalty following the Nazi conquest of Norway and Holland in 1940.

Marion—indeed, everyone at Val Kill, including the hired help—became exceedingly fond of Queen Wilhelmina and Princess Juliana of the Netherlands, and of Juliana's children. They were often at Val Kill Cottage in the warm season, swam much in the pool, lunched and relaxed at teatime on the terrace or in the gardens; and never at any time did they "put on airs." They were completely democratic, not only in manner but in fundamental attitude, Marion believes. Wilhelmina was fond of telling about a drugstore clerk she came to know and like during a summer she spent on Cape Cod. She was delighted when the clerk greeted her, as he invariably did: "Good morning, Queen, and how are you today?" She, her daughter, and her grandchildren became integral and beloved parts of the Val Kill "family"; and when Juliana discovered that she was again in a family way, one of the first persons she told about it at Val Kill was Nellie Johannesen, with whom she had a beautiful rapport. "She stopped at the Val-Kill Teashop one day when Nellie was making jam in the kitchen," says Marion, "and she went out into the kitchen and put her arm around Nellie and just said, with great pride and joy, that she was going to have another baby."

Far different was the case with Crown Princess Martha of Norway. Marion and Nancy did not care for her. "For one thing, she just took over my room in the cottage—kept her things there, without a by-your-leave," Marion complains. "And she never let you forget that she was the crown princess. . . ." She was not actually beautiful when you studied her closely, in Marion's opinion, but she managed somehow to give an impression of great beauty. She was very stylish. She carried herself with regal grace. And she could be very charming when she wished to be, as she did when with FDR; she put herself out to please him, and did please him, becoming one of his favorites. Once FDR asked Marion to look for a house in the Hyde Park neighborhood where the crown princess might establish a home for herself and three children, and Marion insists that she *did* try to find one—but not very hard, and with no success.

160

If there was any change in FDR's personal attitude toward Marion and Nancy as a result of the changed relationship with Eleanor—if there was the slightest diminution of his affection for them—they saw no sign of it. He had certainly been informed of the developing quarrel when Marion, returned from Sweden and England, presented him with a piece of Swedish glass. He thanked her warmly and presented her, in turn, with a tablecloth he had acquired during a summer cruise in the Pacific on the U.S.S. *Houston.* On it were embroidered his initials, hers, and 1938. He continued to involve Marion now and then in his personal political concerns. During the 1940 Democratic National Convention, where Marion served on the Resolutions Committee, he used her as a secret pipeline to him, through Sumner Welles, of information about the Platform Committee's heated argument over foreign policy. It was in part through her that he impressed upon the committee the necessity to modify the plank that isolationists had written into the platform, flatly asserting that the United States would not again engage in a "foreign war"; the modifying phrase, which Marion helped to fight through the committee, was "except in case of attack."

He introduced Winston Churchill to Marion and Nancy when Churchill was staying at the Big House in the blistering hot late June of 1942—and one of Marion's most vivid memories is of the British Prime Minister's first swim in the Val Kill pool.

There was a little bathhouse among the trees below the pool, where swimmers donned their bathing suits. Churchill, wearing a wide-brimmed hat, as he always did for protection against the summer sun, and with a long cigar—as always—in his mouth, entered the bathhouse, accompanied by his secretary. The latter emerged a minute later. "Mr. Churchill has his bathing dress," said the secretary to Marion, "but he would like instead to wear a pair of trunks. Do you have a pair he might wear?" Quite a collection of trunks had been accumulated over the years in the cottage and Marion found a pair she thought might be of adequate girth. The secretary took them into the bathhouse. In a few minutes he was back again. "You wouldn't have a bit of cotton?" he asked. Marion showed her astonishment. "For his ears," the secretary explained. Marion gave him a piece of lamb's wool.

Finally, the Lion of Britain came forth accoutered for his battle with the waves but still wearing his hat, still clamping his cigar between his teeth; and the sight generated in Marion a heightened suspense. Would the cigar and hat accompany the great man into the pool? Paunchy, cherubic ("he looked just like a kewpie doll"), his skin "white as the driven snow," he sauntered to pool's edge, where, at the last possible moment, the hat came off and the cigar was laid carefully down. He jumped into the pool without wetting his head. "He bounced in the water like a rubber ball," swears Marion. "He didn't sink at all." He swam back and forth, climbed out to wrap himself in a huge bath towel provided by Marion, put his hat again upon his head, his cigar again between his teeth, and went over to a grassy spot in the shade of a tree where he sat in silent meditation for a little while. Then he arose and came to Marion, saying he would like a butterfly net! "Well, I couldn't produce a butterfly net nor any substitute for one, so that idea of his, whatever it was—I never discovered what it was—had to be discarded."

A little over a year later, in early September of 1943, Churchill was at Hyde Park for a few days before the opening of the First Quebec Conference. He came over to Val Kill Cottage for a picnic lunch. It didn't occur to Nancy or Marion to serve drinks before a picnic lunch, but they noticed that the Prime Minister became fidgety as he sat waiting for food. At last he "couldn't stand it any longer; he called to Nan and asked her for a bottle." Marion can't remember whether it was brandy or whiskey he asked for, but she does know it was a full bottle. She now has in her possession, therefore, a pictorial record of the astonishing rate of Churchill's alcoholic consumption, for the height of the liquor in the bottle on the table is clearly visible in the successive photographs Nancy took.

FINALE

BY THE TIME of Churchill's first visit to Hyde Park, Marion was sadly approaching the end of her career as a professional educator. Within a few months after her decision to affiliate with Dalton, she regretted it. Todhunter and all that Todhunter had represented in educational theory and practice were simply obliterated. In the late spring of 1942 she withdrew from Dalton. For two years after that she was director of public education for the American Arbitration Association. She was an instructor at Hunter College during the 1944–1945 school term. She was also, in those years, a panel member of the National War Labor Board, Region 2. These were arduous, interesting assignments; but they could not bury beyond all feeling an ache of loss, a sense of things ending that had been so long for her, and Nancy, a source of rich, joyful experience.

Missy suffered a stroke while attending a party in Washington in the summer of 1941. Partially paralyzed, her speech affected, she was never able to resume her duties at the White House. Sara Delano Roosevelt died on September 7 of that same year, and Hall died of cirrhosis of the liver a week or so later. Many of the key figures of the New Deal, who had been much at Hyde Park, no longer came there, having been shunted aside as "Doctor Win-the-War" took over from "Doctor New Deal," as FDR put it. Missy died in the summer of 1944. Gus Gennerich died. "Pa" Watson, the President's beloved appointments secretary, died aboard the ship on which he and FDR's party were returning from the Yalta Conference in February of 1945.

And by then, FDR himself was obviously failing.

Marion's last personal contact with him was at the Big House on the evening of 1944's election day. As they sat together, laughing, she put her hand on his thigh just above his knee and was appalled to feel no flesh there at all. Always before, despite the withering blast of his polio, there had been *some* muscular substance to his legs. Now they were skin and bone.

"But I did not associate death with him," Marion remembers. "Not then. Not ever."

He died on the afternoon of April 12, 1945, at Warm Springs. Marion and Nancy were in the cottage at Val Kill. Next day Marion went over to the Big House to see William Plog ("dear Mr. Plog") who had entered Roosevelt employ as Mrs. Sara Delano Roosevelt's gardener when Franklin was a sixteen-year-old student at Groton, and who had been superintendent of the Hyde Park acres for decades. It was "stupid" of her to come to him, she told Plog, but she wanted to ask him if there were anything at all she could do to help with the preparations for the burial. As a matter of fact there was, Plog said. He had just received a telegram saying that the burial would be not in the churchyard of St. James at Hyde Park village, where James and Sara Delano Roosevelt were buried, but in his mother's rose garden, which Plog himself had helped to lay out in the late 1890s, adjacent to the Big House.

"Come with me and we'll pace out the place together," Plog said.

While they were in the garden an undertaker from Poughkeepsie came up to them to say that he'd been notified of the burial plans. "I'll send my men out this afternoon to dig the grave," he said. That would not be necessary, Plog said. "I think the President would want his own men to do that," he explained, "and we shall do it." Then the undertaker left, and Plog looked again at the telegram he had received. "It says here that his head is to be to the east," he said. "That isn't right. We will put his head to the west. Then he will be looking always east to the rising sun and the coming of a new day."

And that is the way it was done.

166

INDEX

Vireo (sloop), 39
Vittondale Mine, 18, 19

Wagner, Robert F., 64
Walker, James J., 99, 101
Warm Springs (Georgia), 44, 51, 55, 61–64 *passim*, 80–84 *passim*, 90, 111, 129, 166
Warm Springs Foundation, 63
Watson, Edwin T. ("Pa"), 165
Welchpool, 116
Welles, Sumner, 105, 127, 161
Weona II (houseboat), 29

Westfield, New York, 4
Wilhelmina (queen of the Netherlands), 160
Williams, Aubrey, 127
Wilson, M. L., 119, 120, 121
Wilson, Woodrow, 103
Women's Democratic News, 27, 28, 80, 85, 112, 113
Women's Division, New York Democratic Party, 7, 12–13, 15, 26, 79, 85, 90, 122, 144, 146
Women's Trade Union League, 23–24, 85, 90, 91

KENNETH S. DAVIS

A native of Kansas with degrees from Kansas
State University and the University of Wisconsin,
Kenneth S. Davis has been at various times and
places a newspaper reporter, war correspondent,
instructor in journalism, magazine editor, consul-
tant of the U.S. State Department's UNESCO
Relations Staff, and special assistant to a university
president. Since 1959 he and his wife, Florence,
have lived in Princeton, Massachusetts.